OSPREY AIRCRAFT OF THE ACES • 63

Fokker D VII Aces of World War 1
Part 2

SERIES EDITOR: TONY HOLMES

OSPREY AIRCRAFT OF THE ACES • 63

Fokker D VII Aces of World War 1
Part 2

Norman Franks and Greg VanWyngarden

OSPREY
PUBLISHING

Front cover

On the evening of 24 September 1918, Ltn Carl Degelow, CO of *Jagdstaffel* 40, led his pilots against ten Armstrong Whitworth FK 8 bombers of the Royal Air Force's No 82 Sqn, which were in turn being escorted by SE 5a fighters of No 41 Sqn. The black Fokker D VIIs climbed to attack the higher-flying escorts, and the action which ensued was later detailed by Degelow in his memoirs (translated by Peter Kilduff);

'We gained altitude and caught the British SE 5s from the least-expected point – right beneath their floorboards. I closed in on a fellow with a big white "Y" painted on his top wing. This "Mister Y" was a very skilful flier, and he avoided my attack through a series of very deft turns. Nothing I did could entice him to come down to my level. I pulled my Fokker straight up, and for one advantageous moment I had the SE 5 squarely in front of my guns. I pressed the buttons of my machine guns really only to intimidate my partner by the fire, and hopefully get him to give up his advantageous altitude. But, in so doing, some of my shots, which were surely accidental hits, went into the reserve fuel tank of the enemy aircraft. Bright flames immediately burst from the emergency fuel supply on the top wing. I was very pleased by my bluff, and believed the enemy now to be finished.

'"Mister Y" had, however, pulled far away. Then, with his machine glowing with fire, he dived right at me, all the while maintaining a murderous stream of fire from his machine guns. The Englishman suddenly made a violent dive, during which the rush of air almost snuffed out the inferno over his head. After a last futile attack, and recognising the hopelessness of continued fighting, he decided to withdraw, trying to slip away from me. I pursued him doggedly, and was soon joined by another gentleman of my *Staffel* who added a few shots to the effort. Severely battered by our attack, the enemy aircraft exploded at low altitude and broke up close to the edge of Zillebeke Lake'.

Despite Degelow's mistaken assertion, his opponent, Capt C Crawford, somehow survived the destruction of his aircraft to be taken prisoner by German infantry. He had become yet another victim of the superb Fokker D VII (*Cover artwork by Mark Postlethwaite*)

First published in Great Britain in 2004 by Osprey Publishing
Elms Court, Chapel Way, Botley, Oxford, OX2 9LP

ISBN 1 84176 729 8

Edited by Tony Holmes and Bruce Hales-Dutton
Page design by Tony Truscott
Cover Artwork by Mark Postlethwaite
Aircraft Profiles by Harry Dempsey
Index by Glyn Sutcliffe
Scale Drawings by Mark Styling
Origination by Grasmere Digital Imaging, Leeds, UK
Printed in China through Bookbuilders

04 05 06 07 08   10 9 8 7 6 5 4 3 2 1

EDITOR'S NOTE

To make this best-selling series as authoritative as possible, the Editor would be interested in hearing from any individual who may have relevant photographs, documentation or first-hand experiences relating to the world's elite pilots, and their aircraft, of the various theatres of war. Any material used will be credited to its original source. Please contact Tony Holmes via e-mail at:
tony.holmes@osprey-jets.freeserve.co.uk

ACKNOWLEDGEMENTS

The authors wish to thank R Duiven, P M Grosz, A Weaver, G H Williams, S T Lawson, Robert Gill, Dr Volker Koos, H H Wynne, Dr G Merrill, D S Abbott, R Rimell, Dave Roberts, Jörn Leckschied, Volker Haeusler, Dr Dieter H M Gröschel, J Ladek, A van Geeteruyn, Johan Ryheul, Dave Watts, R Kastner, Dr Hannes Taeger and so many others who helped in the compilation of this work. The advice, photos and information provided by eminent historian Alex Imrie were of great value. Gunnar Söderbaum was extremely generous with his expertise on the naval pilots and Wouter Warmoes provided photos from his marvellous *Jasta* 43 collection. Manfred Thiemeyer gave several valuable insights. Thanks are extended to Peter Kilduff for his assistance and permission to quote from *Germany's Last Knight of the Air*. The staff of the History of Aviation Collection at the University of Texas, in Dallas, were always very helpful. Finally, the authors are indebted to O'Brien Browne for supplying translations of German literature.

For details of all Osprey Publishing titles please contact us at:

Osprey Direct UK, P.O. Box 140, Wellingborough, Northants NN8 4ZA, UK
E-mail: **info@ospreydirect.co.uk**

Osprey Direct USA, c/o MBI Publishing, P.O. Box 1, 729 Prospect Ave, Osceola, WI 54020, USA
E-mail: **info@ospreydirectusa.com**

Or visit our website: **www.ospreypublishing.com**

CONTENTS

INTRODUCTION

In *Osprey Aircraft of the Aces 53 - Fokker D VII Aces of World War 1, Part 1* we covered the German Army aces of the *Jagdstaffeln* forming the four *Jagdgeschwadern* equipped with the D VII in 1918. In this second volume, we cover some of the aces in those *Jastas* that were not part of a *Jagdgeschwader*, as well as those German naval aces who flew the D VII.

We should make it clear that a *Jagdgeschwader* was a permanent grouping of a number of *Jastas*. The most famous of these, of course, was JG I, initially commanded by Rittmeister Manfred Freiherr von Richthofen, which comprised *Jagdstaffeln* 4, 6, 10 and 11. These should not be confused with *Jagdgruppen* (*JGr*), which were non-permanent groupings of a number of *Staffeln* which were usually only grouped together for a limited period and (or) for a specific purpose. These units would still be led by a competent leader, however – probably the ranking *Staffelführer* of one of the *jastas* involved – and were also given a unit number such as *Jagdgruppe Nr* 1.

Some of these early groupings were known by a name such as *Jagdgruppe* Houthulst. However, when it is realised that this unit was in existence only between 6 and 16 November 1917 for some local operation in the area that bore its name, it can be seen that many groupings were extremely short-lived. The composition and location of the various *Gruppen* also changed frequently.

Norman Franks and Greg VanWyngarden
February 2004

FOKKERS OVER FLANDERS

By the spring of 1918 many *Jastas* had a variety of aircraft types on strength – mostly the Albatros D III and D V or Va, Pfalz D IIIa and the Fokker Dr I. The arrival of the Fokker D VII in May 1918 gave their hard-pressed pilots a machine of outstanding quality. Robust, manoeuvrable, easy to fly and eventually to be supplied in numbers, it soon became the main German fighter during the final months of World War 1. Many *Staffeln* did not receive a full complement of D VIIs immediately, however. Instead, an allocation of several D VIIs was generally made to each German Army (*Armee*) and small numbers were then assigned to individual units.

The inferior Albatros and Pfalz fighters were generally flown by the newer, less experienced pilots until they were able – if they survived – to progress to a D VII. Bavarian *Jasta* 35, for instance, received six Fokkers on 24 August 1918 and their six oldest machines were exchanged. *Jasta* CO Rudolf Stark decided that the two pilots who were 'the last to join the *Staffel*' would have to wait for the new machines. Examples of the Pfalz D XII, Siemens Schuckert D III and D IV and the Roland D VI fighters would also appear in the war's final year, but these were never as successful, or as numerous, as the much-desired Fokkers.

The D VII had been designed around the established 160 hp Mercedes D III in-line engine. Some operational D VIIs would be powered by the Mercedes D IIIa (about 160-175 hp) but most would use the high-compression Mercedes D IIIaü (generating 180 to 195 hp). Every pilot wanted the 'over-compressed' 185 hp BMW IIIa for his D VII, but there were never enough of these superb engines. The D VII had thick cantilever wings free of wire bracing, an immensely simple yet strong welded steel-tube fuselage and the basic armament of synchronised twin machine-guns. Besides being produced by the Fokker factory at Schwerin, the aircraft was also built by the Albatros Factory at Johannisthal as the D VII (Alb) and the Ostdeutsche Albatros Werke at Schneidemühl as the D VII (OAW).

The D VII proved a formidable opponent for Allied airmen, especially when flown by an experienced pilot. Much of the quality of the German fighter pilots had diminished due to attrition since the heyday of 1917. In addition, it must be stated that the rapid expansion of the *Jastas* in the winter of 1917-18 (the so-called *Amerika Programme,* creating *Jastas* 42 to 80) led to an inevitable decline in the standards of training and fighting efficiency as manpower and supplies were stretched to the limit. However, there were still many young pilots who were quickly able to give a good account of themselves with the new Fokker. The D VII became famous as the only aircraft to be specifically mentioned in the Allied armistice terms.

This volume covers the pilots and units by German Army front. Each army was allocated a section of the front and each was supported by a number of single-seat, two-seat and bomber units. The two-seaters had specific support tasks such as photography, artillery observation and close infantry support. It was the single-seat fighter units which protected their operations and kept the air over the front clear of Allied two-seaters engaged on similar work. While some *Jagdstaffeln,* especially those in *Jagdgruppen,* did move around, they generally remained on the same designated army front.

This chapter details the *Jagdstaffeln* of the German 4th and 6th armies at the northern end of the Western Front. The 4th Army front extended roughly from the Belgian coast at Ostende to the Ypres area. Besides the army *Jagdstaffeln,* the 4th Army units included the *Marine Feld Jagdstaffeln* – naval land-based fighter units. The 6th Army front stretched approximately from Lille to Douai, in north-western France. By 1918 the *Staffeln* in these two armies were generally opposed by RAF squadrons and a few French naval units. From 20 June to mid-August, the British forces in Flanders were augmented by two American Sopwith Camel units, the 17th and 148th Aero Squadrons, under RAF command. The Flanders *Jastas* also encountered aircraft from the small but courageous Belgian *Aviation Militaire.*

4th ARMY - JAGDGRUPPE Nr 6

Jagdgruppe Nr 6 comprised *Jastas* 7, 16b, 20, 40s, 51 and 56 from June to September 1918, and *Jastas* 7, 20, 40s and 51 from October to the end of the war. *Jagdgruppe Nr 6* had been so designated in March 1918. It had previously been known as *Jagdgruppe* Dixmuiden from October 1917 and was commanded by Oblt Hans-Eberhardt Gandert, leader of *Jasta* 51. When Gandert was taken prisoner on September 29, his place as CO was taken by Hptm Erhard Milch from *Flieger Abteilung* (A) 204. Post-war, Milch would rise to be head of Lufthansa and eventually became Göring's deputy with the rank of Generalfeldmarschall in the Luftwaffe.

Jasta 7

By the time the D VII started to arrive, *Jasta* 7 was flying from Ste Marguerite. Josef Jacobs had been CO since August 1917, and he would continue to lead the unit till the Armistice.

This black D VII of *Jasta* 7 was flown by 24-year-old Lt d R Willi Nebgen, who achieved four victories in the summer of 1918 prior to his death in action near Nieppe on 22 October. His personal insignia was the dark green and white band on the black fuselage. Note the rack for flare cartridges beside the cockpit. Eventually, the wings of *Jasta* 7's Fokkers were also painted in the unit's sable colour *(HAC/UTD)*

Born on a farm at Kreuskapelle in May 1894, Jacobs had entered the aviation service pre-war, beginning his training at Bruno Werntgen's flying school. Becoming a pilot, he was flying two-seaters in F. Fl. Abt. 19 by July 1915. Jacobs was given a Fokker Eindecker in 1916, and he scored his first kill on 12 May. Later he flew the Albatros D II with *Jasta* 22 before taking command of *Jasta* 7 in 1917.

Jacobs is rightly associated with the black Fokker Dr I Triplanes he flew in late 1918, but data preserved in his diary indicates that he had received and flown D VII 365/18 by 16 June. He also flew the same machine on 17 and 21 June, and no doubt on other missions better suited to the high-altitude capabilities of a D VII rather than his Triplanes. It is the authors' belief that D VII 365/18 is the machine displaying Jacobs' devil's head emblem seen in a Ste Marguerite line-up photograph.

In the summer of 1918 the seven pilots of the *Jasta's* black D VIIs

Officers of *Jagdgruppe* 6 pose in front of one of Josef Jacobs' black Triplanes of *Jasta* 7 in late 1918. They are, from left to tight, Ltn Raab (adjutant), Ltn d R Karl Plauth (*Jasta* 51CO), Lt d R Jacobs (*Jasta* 7 CO), Hptm Erhard Milch (*Jagdgruppe* CO), Ltn d R Carl Degelow (*Jasta* 40 CO) and Oblt Waldemar von Dazur (*Jasta* 20 CO) *(HAC/UTD)*

encountered many British units, but at times seemed to be fighting a private war with the No 210 Sqn Camels. On 21 June Jacobs, in 365/18, and his wingman Kurt Schönfelder had a long dogfight with 2Lt R G Carr of No 210 Sqn in Camel B7227. The British report of Carr's loss states that he was attacked by four Fokker biplanes. Jacobs wrote;

'This afternoon I had a rather long fight with a Camel. For 28 minutes he tried to attack me. When once he left, Obflgmstr Schönfelder tried to catch him from above, whereupon his water hose was hit and he was forced to land near Menin. The pilot, a lieutenant, was safe and sound and unwounded.'

This represented Schönfelder's 13th victory. Unusually, he was a naval pilot attached to the army. Schönfelder had learned to fly pre-war, and he was already an ace with the *Jasta* by the time the first D VIIs arrived. Scoring regularly with the type, his Fokker was painted black in line with the *Jasta* colour scheme and personalised through the addition of a golden star motif on the fuselage. Schönfelder was Jacobs' most trusted flying mate, and close friend. He usually called him *mein Wassermann* (literally 'my water-bearer'). On 28 May 1918, Schönfelder began a scoring streak, downing five Camels, an SE 5 and two balloons by 21 June, bringing his score to 13. However, on the 26th, *Jasta* 7 tangled once again with No 210 Sqn, and this time it was Schönfelder who was shot down near Bousbecque by aces Kenneth Unger (14 eventual victories), Lawrence Coombes (15) and Ivan Sanderson (11). Jacob's diary recorded;

'Today was an extremely unlucky day for the *Staffel* for I lost my best man, Obflgmstr Schönfelder, in aerial combat. We had taken off for an evening sortie, and in the vicinity of Ypres a squadron of 15 to 20 Englishmen was sighted dropping bombs on our side of the lines. We manoeuvred for position, gaining some altitude, but were immediately jumped by three Sopwith Camels. I blazed away at one of the Camels, which was slowly spiralling down, when I saw a Fokker D VII drop by me with its right top wing disintegrating. He dived vertically and I recognised the Fokker of *Wassermann* by its beautiful golden star.

'Seeing that Schönfelder's aircraft was totally disabled, I had to resume combat with my adversary, who was now in a steep dive towards Menin. As he attempted to straighten out, I jabbed several times with both guns until the wings of the Camel folded up and the wreckage crashed into the ground at the castle gardens in Menin.

Obflgmstr Kurt Schönfelder (right) poses for a souvenir photograph with a captured RAF airman who is still wearing the old RFC 'maternity jacket' tunic. Schönfelder was one of Jacobs' closest comrades, and also one of the best pilots in *Jasta* 7. The D VII seen here may have been his own aircraft, decorated with a golden star *(HAC/UTD)*

'When I arrived there a little later I could only see a small amount of debris and a corpse next to it. This was 19-year-old Lt Boothman of No 210 Sqn RAF, who had so smartly attacked me.'

Three days later, in the gloom of a rainy Flanders day, Schönfelder was laid to rest in Linselles. Jacobs wrote;

'Hptm Wilberg, representing the *Kofl* (*Kommander der Flieger*, the officer in charge of an army's air units), and many gentlemen of many divisions, *Jagdstaffeln* and our entire *Staffel* were present. Schönfelder lay under a large mass of wreaths in a sheet metal and black wood coffin with his golden star, which had always served as the identification of his aircraft. With *Wassermann* gone, I have lost the last of my old *Jasta 7*.'

The RAF squadrons in Flanders soon became very familiar with the flight of black D VIIs led by a black Triplane.

One of the better D VII pilots of *Jasta 7* was Uffz Paul Hüttenrauch, who had been with the unit since early February but had not scored his first victory until July. Between then and the end of the war, he claimed eight kills. By late summer all *Jasta 7* aircraft were painted jet black, individual markings often comprising a pilot's initial on the top wing in white, which was sometimes repeated on the side of the fuselage. An aerial photograph of the *Staffel* airfield shows one such black D VII marked with an 'H' in this manner, which was probably Hüttenrauch's.

Jasta 16b

A Bavarian unit (hence the 'b' in its designation), Jasta 16b probably did not begin to receive D VIIs until August. It was commanded by Oblt Friedrich 'Fritz' Röth, who was born in September 1893 in Nuremberg (Nürnburg). A former artilleryman, he was wounded early in the war and spent some time in hospital. Commissioned in May 1915 following his recovery, Röth transferred to the aviation service but was then injured in a crash so he did not become a pilot until early 1917. Flying two-seaters with Fl. Abt. (A) 296b, he won the Bavarian Military Merit Order 4th Class in June. Röth then became a fighter pilot with *Jasta 23b*, gaining ten victories, before being appointed its leader.

Röth was an airmen with a penchant for 'balloon-busting'. Indeed, of his first 15 victories, all but one were 'sausages'. Often they were scored in batches – four on the evening of 1 April 1918 and five in the late afternoon of 29 May. By the time the D VII arrived, his tally stood at 18, and between then and the war's finale, he brought his score to 28 victories. These included six more balloons, in two batches of three, scored on the evenings of 13 August and 10 October 1918. Röth was not considered a good marksman, and this apparently

A smiling Fritz Röth (right) of *Jasta 16b* is seen with two fellow Bavarian fighter aces, *Jagdgruppe* 8 leader Hptm Eduard von Schleich (centre) and *Jasta 23b* CO Oblt Otto Kissenberth (with dachshund). In the background is Kissenberth's Roland D VIb. Both Schleich and 'balloon-buster' Röth achieved their final victories flying the Fokker, but Kissenberth probably never flew the type

led him to specialise in balloons because they were large targets. However, he still managed to shoot down eight aircraft.

'Röth was not a braggart nor a rough fighter by nature, but was mild, gentle, humane and an idealist in the truest sense. He was also a soldier, an officer of unusually high devotion to duty, with the courage of a "dare devil".'

These were the compliments paid by Ltn Max Gossner, Röth's *Jasta* 23b squadron comrade and later *Jasta* 77b CO. Röth came from a deeply religious family and was a devout believer, sometimes troubled by the lives he took in combat. He received the *Ordre Pour le Mérite* on 9 September. On 10 October he wrote to his friend Gossner;

'Warm thanks for all of your greetings. After the *Pour le Mérite*, I was sent home on leave for 14 days by the *Kofl*. I would have much preferred to travel during bad weather, but nevertheless it was quite nice to be home again. The day before yesterday I shot down an *Infanterieflieger* (infantry support flier) as my 24th. Since then I have brought back my Fokker a few times with various hits. Jacobs has 38, Degelow 26! We are still flying on the same front, however we belong to another *Gruppe*. Have changed airfields much. Gandert is missing.'

Four days later Röth was wounded in the foot while shooting down a DH 9 for his 28th kill, which was also the 82nd, and final, victory of *Jasta* 16b – he had scored the lion's share of *Staffel* claims in late 1918. On 11 November Röth made one final flight as a passenger in a two-seater flown by *Staffel* pilot Max Holtzem, who later recalled;

'We flew until noontime. Röth, with his leg in a cast, had asked me to show him the frontline in a last flight. His doctor had forbidden him to fly, but he went anyway. He was heartbroken about this ending, and now there was revolution in Germany'.

After the demobilisation of *Jasta* 16b in Cologne (Köln), Röth returned to his home city of Nuremberg. Overcome by depression, and some say, guilt over the men he killed in the war, he committed suicide on New Year's Eve 1918. He was posthumously awarded the Knight's Cross of the Military Max-Joseph Order in 1919, which gave him the title Ritter von Röth.

Jasta 20

Ltn Joachim von Busse had commanded *Jasta* 20 since December 1917, the unit probably receiving its first D VIIs during July 1918. Von Busse, who was a former *Jäger* officer from Hohensalzen, was born in May 1893 and transferred to the aviation service in March 1915. Following the usual period on two-seaters – Fl. Abt. 12 and KG 4 – he moved to *Jasta* 3 in August 1917. With four victories, von Busse was made CO of *Jasta* 20 and scored his next three kills in July 1918 before being wounded on 1 August. Returning to his command, he took his score to 11 by November, most probably with the D VII. Von Busse received the Knight's Cross of the Royal Hohenzollern House Order, which was often known simply as 'the Hohenzollern'.

Ltn Karl Plauth, from Munich, was born on 27 August 1896. He had suffered a wound serving with a pioneer regiment on the Verdun Front in 1916, winning the Iron Cross, 1st Class in the process. Plauth then transferred to aviation, serving in two-seaters in Fl. Abt. (A) 204 before

Karl Plauth scored his first ten victories flying the D VII with *Jasta* 20 and was then appointed *Jasta* 51 CO after little more than three months as a *jagdflieger*! He survived the war with a victory tally of 17

Jasta 40 plays host to reluctant RAF guests after their successful combats of 14 July 1918. Having spent time in Texas and Chicago, CO Carl Degelow spoke English and always enjoyed socialising with British prisoners. They are, from left: unknown, Ltn Frodien, Ltn d R Willi Rosenstein, Gftr Ebert (in rear), Lt N H Marshall of No 85 Sqn (with bandaged nose), Ltn Hermann Gilly, Lt E M Garrett of No 64 Sqn (in the old RFC 'maternity jacket' and thigh boots), Degelow and Ltn Hans Jeschonnek. Two groundcrewmen lay in front of the group. Four SE 5a victories were claimed by *Jasta* 40 that day, two by Degelow (his 10th and 11th kills), Rosenstein (his fourth) and Gilly (his third). Hans Jeschonnek achieved two confirmed victories in World War 1, and in World War 2 he rose to the rank of Generaloberst and Luftwaffe Chief of Staff, before committing suicide in 1943 *(R Gill)*

commencing fighter pilot training. He was then assigned to *Jasta* 20 on 14 June 1918 and began flying the D VII, with which, by late September, he had accumulated ten victories. Some of Plauth's articulate writings have survived, here translated by O'Brien Browne;

'9 July 1918 – My first victory, a SPAD single-seater. The story hasn't quite been cleared up yet. On this morning the *Staffel* shot down four – one each for Ltn von Busse, von Dazur, von Decker and me. Decker and I each have one on this side of the lines, but we both could not observe the impact because we immediately had aerial fights with other single-seaters. How such an aerial fight happens in front of you is difficult to describe. The main thing here is to get in close, then one always has success. During this victory, I shot from 25 m with both machine-guns.

'14 July – Yesterday, aerial battle in the usual way. I lost the vertical controls and tail fin from my Fokker. Still came down all right and got caught up in a wire entanglement. Of course, a wonderful crash, almost in a crater field. The Fokker is totally done for. I have a black eye and my forehead had to be stitched up somewhat. Tomorrow, I hope to be rid of this bandage. My concern is now only with a new Fokker, as I have, despite great enthusiasm, no desire to fly an Albatros or a Pfalz at the Front. I have just been to the eye ward and had myself put back into shape there. The only thing I am sorry about is, again, having to sit out these eight days.'

Plauth soon discovered that his right eye had been damaged more severely than previously thought, and he hoped the scar tissue would not affect his sight permanently. He would soon recover enough to return to flying D VIIs in combat once again, but not without recalling a common German pilot's superstition on 17 July;

'One should never have his machine photographed, and above all not himself. Usually, there is a crash afterwards. This time it was once again true, as a thousand times already. Is that not strange?'

Later he wrote;

'25 July – I already have five front flights behind me. My flesh wound has healed without a trace, the injury to the outer cornea as well. I still cannot see as clearly with this eye as earlier.

'26 July – This morning I had a very fine aerial battle with a Sopwith in which he never hit me. I succeeded in shooting at him very well. But I wasn't quick enough and shot off my entire ammunition supply too rashly so that finally he got over the lines – he would have been finished with 10 or 20 shots! But then both machine guns broke down. However, with every flight one learns. I myself have received engine damage from ground-based machine gun fire – most likely from our own infantry.

'17 August – Today my fifth, an SE 5 English single-seater north of Werwik. Pilot dead. Happily, the pilot of the fourth one, which burned, is not dead but only wounded and in the hospital. He complained that I had kept firing until the very end. Actually, I would like to visit him and explain to him why I had shot for so long. They always want to try to get away, and this one can only block by forcing the opponent to continually bank.

'15 September – Today the first flight to the front after my leave. Seven to ten SE 5s attacked from above. Hobein had a jam and I attempted to finish up with seven SE 5s at which, however, I thoroughly failed. I tried to fight while banking but could not get above the gentlemen. I stood on my nose and took off. While doing this, my shot-up upper wing tore and I had to creep home very carefully and also arrived in good order. Anyway, I am totally thankful that it turned out this way, and am actually happy to be brought down a notch, which protects one from arrogance.

'16 September – This morning, between Armentières and Roubaix-Tourcoing, my seventh, a de Havilland two-seater from a squadron of bombers. The landing gear was unscathed because it preferred to land on its back. During the aerial fight, the observer had already fallen out of the aircraft, dead. The pilot was perhaps already unconscious. He is also dead. This victory was relatively easy. One only had to attack and get in close. The observer, who had shot at me at the beginning, put no hits into me. I cut out a piece of the cockade and want to keep it. If I am successful in getting several more victories, I will perhaps be on the way to *Staffelführer*. The easiest and most comfortable thing for me would be to remain a pilot.

'21 September – Today I succeed in getting my eighth, a de Havilland, shot out from a strong bomber squadron. This time I needed a rather long time until I finally forced him to give up the fight. I had lots of jams. The Englishman noticed this and continuously attempted to get away. After the first seconds of the attack, the situation was already safe for me. I immediately shot up the observer's machine gun so that he was defence-less. This time I did not keep shooting until he was lying below. I wanted him to land smoothly once I had recognised his intention to go down on our side. He floated out correctly, too, but then, right above the ground, he began, for unknown reasons, to catch fire and totally burned upon impact.

'As far as I could tell I had not seriously wounded the observer, as he was at least still alive shortly before landing and was waving to his pilot. So, then, all the more so this sad ending affected me.'

Like many of his fellow pilots, Karl Plauth had a superstitious fear of allowing himself, or his aircraft, to be photographed before a flight. He disregarded this when he posed here with his 7th *Jasta* 20 victory – a DH 9 shot down near Lille on 16 September. His victim may have been No 103 Sqn's D489, flown by 2Lt W H Cole (pilot) and Sgt S Hookway, both of whom were killed

On 30 September, Plauth was named acting *Staffelführer* of *Jasta* 51, also in *Jagdgruppe Nr 6*.

Ltn Johannes Gildemeister of *Jasta* 20 gained five victories in 1918, the last three or four with the D VII. One of these, scored on 17 August, was over the Canadian ace W G Claxton DSO DFC of No 41 Sqn RAF, who had achieved 37 kills before being wounded and taken prisoner.

Jasta 40s

Like *Jasta* 7, Saxon *Jagdstaffel* 40 decorated its machines with a black fuselage, although with a completely white tail section, its leader's machine bearing the famous white stag emblem. The *Staffel* commander was Carl Degelow, from Müsterdorf, who was born in January 1891. Pre-war, he had worked in the USA as an industrial chemist, and therefore spoke English well. Degelow returned to Germany shortly before the outbreak of war to

enlist in the second *Nassauischen Infanterie-Regiment* Nr 88, seeing action in France and Russia. Commissioned in July 1915, he transferred to the aviation service the following year and was sent to Fl. Abt. (A) 216 on the Somme at the beginning of 1917.

Degelow's aggressive flying got him moved to fighters, and *Jasta* 7, and by mid-May 1918 he had scored a handful of victories prior to his transfer to *Jasta* 40. After the death, on 9 July, of previous leader Helmuth Dilthey, Degelow took over the unit. He survived the war to write a short memoir, *Mit dem weissen Hirsch durch dick und dünn* (*With the White Stag through Thick and Thin*). In 1979, nine years after Degelow's death, historian Peter Kilduff expanded on this work, using extensive interviews and additional material to produce *Germany's Last Knight of the Air*, which provides an excellent view of 4th Army D VII operations.

Degelow picked up his first D VII on 25 June 1918. After having *Staffel* mechanics check it over and load the ammunition, he took it up for a brief hop. During this 'test flight' Degelow encountered a scrap between Camels and D VIIs of another *Jasta* and downed a Sopwith attacking one of the Fokkers – it was his sixth victory. Degelow's claims from July onwards were attained

Degelow (fourth from right in light-coloured tunic) is pictured with his pilots in front of their black *Jasta* 40 warbirds. The first five D VIIs from the right may be identified as being those of Degelow, with its stag and white diagonal stripe on the upper wing, Rosenstein's, with a white chord-wise stripe, Jeschonnek's with a rampant bull, Gilly's, with its white swastika, and Frodien's, with a hawk's head *(R Gill)*

Carl Degelow celebrates his award of the Knight's Cross of the Royal Hohenzollern House Order, seen above his left tunic pocket, and is pictured here with his 'white stag' D VII. The stag has golden yellow hooves and antlers. The pale rib tapes are quite evident on the five-colour fabric wing covering and a tubular gunsight is mounted between the guns *(Robert Gill)*

with the D VII, six aircraft falling to his guns in that first month. He was on leave in August, but added six more victories in September, ten in October and one – his 30th and last – on 4 November. Degelow wrote the following account of his successes over a group of SE 5 fighters on a bombing mission on 14 July;

'We were flying over Lys when I became aware that far behind the British lines a big formation of enemy machines was approaching our positions. Even at this great distance I could make out that the enemy force consisted of about 20 single-seat fighters. I held back our attack until the enemy squadron made a turn. Then we could hit the gentlemen on the outermost flank who were straining to keep up. At my signal – waggling my wings – *Jasta* 40 charged into the crowd of SE 5 fighters and each man picked out an adversary.

'I side-slipped with my "dancing partner" who, as the first shots hit his aeroplane, was forced out of the fray. Apparently the Englishman had hopes of gliding back to his own lines but that was something I did not care for as I always placed great value in personally meeting an opponent after an aerial contest. I made my viewpoint known with a burst of machine gun fire just ahead of him. The Tommy turned in a direction more to my liking and then landed. On greeting the soft earth of Flanders, however, his aircraft turned over. Then the pilot crawled out from beneath the wreckage. I immediately spotted him from the air as he was wearing a marvellously stylish bright yellow leather coat.'

After seeing the British pilot taken prisoner by artillery troops, Degelow started for home, only to discover one of his guns had jammed;

'Just then I was taken by surprise when a series of shots came up from the ground. I spotted the object of the ground gunners' attention – a single British gentleman far below me, dropping bombs. Having cleared the jam in my guns, I went after him with a roar. I then underwent what was perhaps the most bitter dogfight of my life. This Tommy was so wild that whenever we flew toward each other he tried to ram me. We repeatedly whizzed past each other with only metres to spare.

'Now each of us tried to overtake the other in a turn and then get the opponent in his gunsight. After a quarter of an hour of fighting, my partner then tried his utmost to disappear from the scene. I got right on his tail. During the ensuing chase, ever closer to the ground, as my opponent tried every trick to shake me off, I succeeded in bringing him down with a well-aimed stream of fire. We were just within the advance British lines when, from about 50 m altitude, and with the engine going full out, the enemy aircraft dived furiously into the ground and on impact was smashed to pieces.'

Degelow's first opponent, who was captured, was probably Lt N H Marshall of No 85 Sqn RAF. On return to his base Degelow learned that Willi Rosenstein and Hermann

High spirits in the *Jasta* 40 Officer's *Kasino* as the *Staffelführer* is placed under severe 'threat'. Seated, from left to right, are Hermann Gilly, Carl Degelow, Hans Jeschonnek, Willy Rosenstein and Frodien *(R Gill)*

Gilly of his *Jasta* had also scored against the SE 5 formation (Nos 85 and 64 Sqns RAF), bringing the *Staffel* tally to four for the day, although only three SE 5s were actually lost.

Rewarded with the 'Hohenzollern', Degelow then became the last German soldier of the war to receive the *Pour le Mérite*, on 9 November. In World War 2 he served as a major in the Luftwaffe and died in Hamburg on 9 November 1970 – the 52nd anniversary of the award of his 'Blue Max'.

Hermann Gilly was another pilot to gain victories with the D VII. He had been born in Donaueschingen in 1894 and joined *Infanterie-Regiment Nr* 168 after the outbreak of the war. He was commissioned on the Eastern Front in March 1916, then transferred to the aviation service in November. A year later he was serving as a pilot in Fl. Abt. (A) 204 on the Piave Front in Italy. Gilly joined *Jasta* 40s in April 1918 and, except for a brief spell in *Jasta* 29, stayed with this unit till war's end.

His D VII displayed a large good luck swastika in white and became respected by his adversaries and comrades alike. Degelow recorded that a captured RAF airman given a tour of the *Jasta* 40s airfield had pointed out Gilly's Fokker and said, 'We know this one very well. We call him the "double lucky stick"'. On 14 July 1918, the famous ace 'Mick' Mannock of No 85 Sqn attacked a D VII, which he described as having a black fuselage, white tail and a swastika in white. This may well have been Gilly. If so, he survived the encounter. Gilly only scored his last three victories in the D VII, but it brought his score to seven. He too served as a major in the Luftwaffe during World War 2.

Ltn d R Willi Rosenstein ended the war with eight (possibly nine) victories, the last five or six scored while flying the D VII. From Stuttgart, Rosenstein was born on 28 January 1892 of Jewish parents. Always fascinated by engines, he became a pilot in 1912 and gained some measure of fame as a pre-war airman and flight instructor. After the war began Rosenstein soon entered military aviation and joined Fl. Abt. 19 in March 1915. His first victories were scored with *Jasta* 27 in September 1917, often flying with the CO, Hermann Göring. At the end of 1917 he requested a transfer from this unit due to a quarrel with Göring over some anti-Semitic remarks made by the *Staffelführer*. Rosenstein's third victory was consequently scored in *Kest* 1a, a home defence unit.

He moved to *Jasta* 40 at the beginning of July 1918, just as it was re-equipping with new Fokkers. He would become Degelow's trusted flying mate and second in command and flew in the 'tail end charlie' position in *Staffel* patrols. As Degelow said, he was, 'keeping the rear free of our enemies as he flew last and highest in our formation'.

Rosenstein finished the war with *Jasta* 40. He had been recommended for the 'Hohen-zollern' but did not receive it due to the Armistice. With the rise of

Willy Rosenstein's Albatros-built D VII is prepared for flight. Note the long gunsight ahead of the pilot. Rosenstein's machine was decorated with a white heart, which Degelow said, 'clearly indicated a good relationship with the eternal woman'. Degelow described Rosenstein as 'my most able colleague, my second-in-command at *Jasta* 40' *(R Gill)*

the Nazis his family emigrated to South Africa in 1936. After World War 2 began, he was, ironically, interned by the South African government as an 'enemy alien', but his son Ernest became a fighter pilot with the South African Air Force. In a final sad irony, Ernest was killed in action over Italy in April 1945. Willy Rosenstein himself died in a flying accident in May 1949.

Jasta 51

Hans-Eberhardt Gandert's *Staffel* 51, also based at Ste Marguerite, may have received its first Fokkers in June 1918. Gandert himself had three victories by this date, and he added five more in June, July and August. Born in Sandberg in September 1892, he was another former *Jäger* and was commissioned in June 1913. Learning to fly immediately before the war, he saw action in two-seaters on the Eastern Front, where he was shot down on 10 October 1914 but managed to walk home. Gandert continued serving with various two-seater units until well into 1917, when he transferred to fighters, gaining his first two victories flying single-seaters with Fl. Abt. 24 in Rumania. Just after Christmas 1917 he was sent to France to take command of *Jasta* 51.

A month after being awarded the 'Hohenzollern', Gandert was shot down in his D VII on 29 September. It is possible that No 210 Sqn was responsible or, as he was attacking British balloon lines, he may have been the victim of ground fire. In any case, he was wounded and taken prisoner. Gandert joined the Luftwaffe in the 1930s and held various training commands during World War 2, retiring in February 1945 with the rank of generalmajor. He died in Augsburg in July 1947.

Following his loss, Gandert was succeeded as leader of *Jasta* 51 by Karl Plauth from *Jasta* 20, who had to assume his new position just as the *Jasta* was changing airfields, retreating from Rumbeke to Menin. He wrote;

'9 October – Shot down my 14th opponent. My name will probably be submitted for the "Hohenzollern". Even though I would be very pleased about this – to have it as a memento of this time – this is definitely not the main thing for me. Leading a *Staffel* in the air pleases me very much now because now I can fly all-out, as I see fit. I have many beginners in the *Staffel* but everything will turn out all right. Two months ago I myself was still a beginner. Now we wish for a few fine days. Before the Englishmen are able to easily triumph over us, their life should be made quite difficult.

'12 October – After four years of brave defence against massive superiority, the homeland appears to have collapsed.

'22 October – After many rainy days, once again good weather this morning in which I shot down on our side of the lines a French two-seater north of Deinze. The aircraft exploded in the air. The victory is thus indisputable. In the *Staffel* I now also slowly have more support from the remaining pilots, who naturally first had to be made aware of my style of flying. There is now a kind of war of movement, unfortunately to the rear instead of forward.'

Plauth scored seven victories in October to bring his score to 17. After the war he continued his studies and activities in aviation, becoming a glider pilot and an engineer with Junkers. Karl Plauth, happiest when his opponents survived, was to die in a flying accident on 1 November 1927.

Jasta 56

Jasta 56 apparently began receiving its first D VIIs soon after May 1918. As *Staffelführer,* Ltn Dieter Collin was a veteran ace who had served in *Jasta* 2 under the great Oswald Boelcke. He then went on to *Jasta* 22, with whom he had scored six victories by 29 March 1918. Collin took command of *Jasta* 56 in April 1918, made four claims in May and three more in July, taking his score to 13. However, on 13 August he was shot down and killed in combat with No 204 Sqn Camels, Capt A J B Tonks (12 kills) and Lt H W M Cumming being credited with his demise over Armentières. Pulled from the wreckage of his Fokker, Collin was rushed to the nearest hospital but died soon after arrival. The Camel pilots did not see the actual crash, so they only claimed an 'out of control' victory.

Ltn Ludwig 'Lutz' Beckmann, from Westphalia, took Collin's place. Joining *Jasta* 56 in March 1918, he too had a lot of experience, having flown with *Jastas* 6 and 48. Beckmann had not, however, scored any victories. By the time the first D V IIs were issued to the unit in May, he had claimed two or three kills, and he quickly found his feet with the new Fokker fighter. Beckmann's score had risen to eight by 5 September, his victims including RAF aces H T Mellings DSC (15 kills) and H A Patey DFC (11 kills), both of No 210 Sqn. Beckmann served in the Luftwaffe in World War 2, being awarded the *Ritterkreuz* in 1942.

Ltn Franz Piechulek was *Jasta* 56's other ace. He had earlier served on home defence duties and in *Jasta* 41 before moving to his last posting in January 1918. By the time the Fokker was in evidence, Piechulek had six victories, and he went on to make this 14 by the war's end. His last victory, on 4 October, was scored over a Belgian Hanriot flown by Sgt Martin of the 11me *Escadrille de Chasse.*

'Lutz' Beckmann, *Jasta* 56 *Staffelführer,* is pictured with his Albatros-built D VII, displaying the unit colours of light blue-grey fuselage, red nose and tail. The red band aft of the cockpit was his personal identification, and it would later bear an additional white wavy 'snake-line'

MFJ I

Also making a significant contribu-tion to the 4th Army's D VII force, German *Marine* (naval) land-based fighter pilots had originally been fighting their own war up along, or just inland from, the North Sea coast since 1916, when two *Kampfeinsitzer Kommandos* (single-seater units) were combined into *Marine-Feldflieger Abteilung* II at Neumünster.

On 1 February 1917 this unit was renamed the *Marine Feld Jasta* (later

'Lutz' Beckmann strikes a Napoleonic pose with his *Jasta* 56 Fokker, now with its fuselage band applied in the red and white colours of his native Westphalia. Beckmann appears to be wearing captured British flying gear

Ltn zur See Gotthard Sachsenberg was a unique and indispensable figure in the development of German land-based World War 1 naval fighter aviation. Appointed to command the *Marine Feld Jagdstaffel* when it was formed on 1 February 1917, he would go on to lead the naval *Jagdgruppe* and eventually the *Marine-Jagdgeschwader Flandern* in late 1918. When Sachsenberg received the *Pour le Mérite* he was 26, and clearly possessed great leadership qualities as well as indisputable skill as a fighter pilot *(Johan Ryheul)*

In some ways the naval equivalent of von Richthofen, Sachsenberg led the *Marine Jagdgeschwader* in this flamboyantly-decorated Fokker. The fuselage displays MFJ chequered yellow and black colours, while the uppersurface of the top wing is probably also yellow, with the (possibly) black patches seen here positioned over the spars probably evidence of some repair or strengthening in the centre-section area. This part of the D VII's wing was prone to structural failure during stressful combat manoeuvres *(Johan Ryheul)*

numbered 'I') and was commanded by Ltn zur See Gotthard Sachsenberg. When the *Marine Jagdgruppe Flandern* was formed from MFJ I and II in October 1917, Sachsenberg also commanded that formation. On 23 June 1918, MFJ III was added to the *Jagdgruppe*. In addition, a fighter-equipped unit known as the *Seefrontstaffel Flandern* (*Seefrosta*) was flying D VIIs in the summer of 1918, and this was divided into two *Ketten* (flights) or *Staffeln*, which became MFJ IV and V in September.

The naval units began receiving Fokker biplanes in June 1918, with the first recorded D VII to be assigned to MFJ I being 427/18, which arrived on the 12th. Seven more were flown in four days later. In mid October 1918, the five naval *Jastas* were permanently combined into the *Marine-Jagdgeschwader Flandern* under Sachsenberg's command, giving him control of some 50 fighters.

All MFJ Fokkers were marked with yellow cowlings and tails, each individual *Jasta* eventually being identified by differing black markings on the yellow elevators.

A former sea cadet, Gotthard Sachsenberg was born in Dessau on 6 December 1891. His first experience of flying was as a Fähnrich zur See (observer). In 1916 Sachsenberg undertook pilot training and eventually flew Fokker Eindeckers. He was given command of MFJ on 1 February 1917 and on 1 May Sachsenberg opened his account by downing a Belgian Farman and Sopwith 1¹/2 Strutter. The majority of his combats were against Royal Naval Air Service aircraft raiding towns along the coast like Zeebrugge and Ostend, or inland targets such as Bruges. By 20 August 1917, with his tally standing at six kills, Sachsenberg won the 'Hohenzollern'. He continued to score steadily, and by 17 June 1918 had 15 victories.

One of the best days of the war for Sachsenberg and his fellow naval pilots was 12 August 1918, when they claimed seven victories. 'Willy' Thöne of MFJ I opened the scoring with a Camel claimed at 0845 hrs. At about 1130 hrs a patrol of five No 204 Sqn Camels was attacked by an equal group of *Seefrosta* D VIIs. Two of the Sopwiths were shot down into the sea, with Lt B Hill killed and Lt S C Askins surviving a swim to be taken prisoner. Thöne also claimed another Camel at this time, which may not have been confirmed. An hour later a formation of No 218 Sqn DH 9s, escorted by Camels of the American 148th Aero Squadron, were intercepted by the D VIIs of MFJ I and the *Seefrosta*. A series of deadly combats ensued.

The 148th pilots reported that the Fokkers had 'black-and-yellow chequered tails' – a perfectly plausible impression of the naval unit colours. Lt R D Gracie died when his Camel was shot to pieces by Sachsenberg, the aircraft losing its wings and falling into the sea. Besides Gracie, three more 148th pilots were wounded, with 1Lt H

Sachsenberg's chequered D VII is seen in the background of this picture of Fokker E V 160/18, which arrived at MFJ I on 10 August 1918. Just visible to the right of the groundcrewman is the single black stripe on the yellow elevator, which identified MJF I aircraft *(HAC/UTD)*

Aldermann probably being the victim of Gerhard Hubrich of the *Seefrosta*. Sachsenberg was additionally credited with one of the DH 9s, taking his score to 21. Osterkamp of MFJ II received credit for another Camel later that day, and claimed two more unconfirmed aircraft.

The pilots of the 148th and No 204 Sqn achieved some revenge the very next day when they cooperated with the Camels of Nos 210 and 213 Sqns in a well-organised bombing and strafing raid on the base of MFJs I, II and III at Jabbeke, which the British called Varsenaere. According to German accounts, the MFJ units had two fighters burned, ten aircraft destroyed and a further five machines damaged. Two pilots were killed and three wounded, with more casualties among the ground personnel.

During the last months of the war, Sachsenberg continued scoring in his yellow and black chequered D VII, raising his total to 31 – his successes won him the *Pour le Mérite* on 5 August. His last victories came after he had returned from leave around 8 October and taken command of the *Marine-Jagdgeschwader*. Ltn z S Phillip Becht (three victories) took over MFJ I when the *Geschwader* was formed.

Shortly after the war Sachsenberg formed and led *Kampfgeschwader Sachsenberg*, which was a large *Freikorps* formation formed to fight the Red Army in the Baltic states. Among the other wartime pilots in this group were Osterkamp, Zenses, Goerth, Scharon and Josef Jacobs. Later, Sachsenberg, who passed away in 1961, held important positions with the Junkers company. His younger cousin Heinz gained 104 victories as a fighter pilot with JG 52 during World War 2.

Another successful MFJ I Fokker pilot was Vzflgmstr d R der Marine-infanterie (MI-naval infantry) Wilhelm 'Willy' Thöne. He was born on 22 January 1893 and joined the navy in 1913, serving on board ship as a machinist. After the outbreak of war he switched to the naval infantry, fighting in Flanders from 1914 to 1917. After becoming a pilot with *Seeflieger-Abteilung* II, Thöne served as an instructor for a while, then joined MFJ I in May 1918. His first kill came on 30 May when he downed a 'SPAD two-seater' over the Nieuport Mole. It was officially confirmed as his fourth victory five months later. Willy Thöne ended the war with perhaps four confirmed kills and one more 'forced to land', with

This photograph of naval pilot Wilhelm Thöne has been heavily retouched. 'Willy' Thöne was a successful MFJ I D VII exponent, claiming several RAF Camels in the summer of 1918. In later years he stated that he had scored 11 confirmed victories, but records covering only about five have been found to date

possibly several more unconfirmed. He recorded an incident that took place on 31 July (translated by O'Brien Browne);

'Shortly before mid-day, our first *Kampstaffel* took off, of which I led one of the two *Ketten* (flights) to patrol over the front. While we were slowly climbing on our side, we saw over there among the streaks of ground fog many enemy fighter flights climbing up from their fliers' nests which were well known to us. But our search was mainly concerned with a large squadron of bombers that had been reported.

After a good half-hour, we had climbed above 6000 m and followed our course along the sea over Ostende to the front. The enemy anti-aircraft fire did not disturb us because their shots exploded far below us as usual.

'The many cumulus clouds at a height of 5000 m made long-distance visibility especially difficult. This was a great advantage to the enemy, and however much we scoured the whole sky, we could not locate the bombers. Rather, the enemy fighter flights continued to come disquietingly nearer. A few had already overtaken us. It would have been madness if we had taken up battle over enemy territory with our 11 machines against more than 50 opponents. Therefore, we swung around over Furnes towards the east, closely followed by the English flights which were simultaneously attempting to pinch us off.

'The situation was becoming extremely critical when another enemy flight came directly at us from the German side. Obviously they wanted to block our way home. Luckily, they had misjudged the height and lay 100 m lower than us. With every second our combat situation could only worsen, so the decision suddenly occurred to me to dive vertically down on the flight coming through under us. I drew a bead on the leader's machine, for whom it was imperative to escape immediately by diving if he didn't want to be rammed. Hardly 50 m back, I roared behind him. With the first bursts from both of my machine guns, the opponent went over lightning fast into a spinning dive. I had to use the same tactics immediately, and by doing this was at the same instant protected from the rattling machine guns of his comrades who were behind me.

'My entire attention was on staying on the opponent's back. Besides this I only heard the singing and whistling of my machine rushing downwards. My *Staffel* comrades told me later that three opponents had immediately attached themselves to me – these were followed by two pilots from my *Kette*. It was a grand sight – approximately 15 machines, alternately friend and enemy, closely pressed together in a speeding dive. Luckily, I knew nothing of this, otherwise I would perhaps have let my opponent escape. After about 2000 m we were finally alone. The man in front of me suddenly did a trick to take away my advantage of height, but I had not fallen for such a trick in a long time. Now it turned into a banking fight.

'I immediately noticed that my opponent at least matched me as a flier, but my Fokker D VII was a bit faster and above all better in climbing than the Sopwith single-seater. From his three pennants I further recognised that I was dealing with a great ace – at least a flight leader. In single combat with an experienced fighter pilot, hits are devilishly difficult to score because of the extraordinary manoeuvres. With my better machine I was, though, successful in continually pushing the Englishman farther over and down above the German sector. If I could first have him near the ground, so I thought, then he must, for better or worse, fly straight and easily become my prey if he did not voluntarily land and become a prisoner.

'In 15 minutes we had come down to the ground. My opponent was sometimes so close to the ground that his undercarriage knocked down sheaves of grain. I was literally hanging on his heels but always, again and again, when I settled myself behind him for a shot, I got into his prop-wash and had, for my own safety, to immediately go to the side or upwards.

'The Tommy understood how to use the tree-lined avenues and tree-edged canals, and thus to steadily get nearer to his own lines. Lower than the tops of the trees, he raced along their rows. Sometimes he even darted through the larger gaps. I had been an instructor for a while at a combat pilot school and was definitely counted among the most skilled pilots, but I couldn't have demonstrated this. Yet I could imitate it because I did not want to be shaken off.

'Thus we went continually westward and were over the large Flanders flood plain from which only isolated trees and bushes stuck out. All of a sudden, a somewhat strange feeling came over me – that I no longer knew the lay of the lines in which I, in the first years of the war, had lain as an infantryman, and that in the rush I had utterly lost my orientation.

'Finally the ground was dry again and we were over the Allied lines. Once again I opened fire with both guns. Strangely, the Tommy no longer cared about this, but stubbornly flew straight ahead. Most likely the last nervous tension had left him once he was again over his own lines.

'Now I could, in barely two or three seconds, adjust my machine in a moment of peace and then watch my tracers disappearing into the middle of the opponent's fuselage. His machine immediately rushed down towards the ground from just about ten metres high and there turned over in a giant fountain of earth. At the same instant I yanked my Fokker up and away from this sight and raced to the flood plain again. My fuel could not last for much longer. In spite of this hard-fought victory, my feelings of triumph were dampened by the recognition of my own situation.

'I had just arrived over the surface of the water when the tack-tack-tack of a trench machine gun was audible behind me, which I immediately recognised as Belgian. I had made a great mistake and flown back the same way, but before I could change direction my engine stopped – probably the carburettor or its lines had been shot up. My first thoughts before the machine's impact were, should I loosen the shoulder straps or not? Now, a few hundred metres before me, trenches were appearing. I had great worries that they too could be enemy ones, so I dived my machine into the water.'

Thöne was thrown clear of his aircraft after his shoulder straps broke, landing unhurt in the deep flood water. After a trying period of swimming and wading, he found his way to a German infantry unit. He finally made

MFJ I ace Bertram Heinrich poses for a convenient photo opportunity with Siemens Schuckert Werke D IV 3028/18. Heinrich claimed nine victories prior to being shot down and killed in a Fokker D VII on 31 August 1918

it back to his *Geschwader* late that evening, having been given up for dead.

As noted, Thöne played a part in the successes of 12 August, using D VII (OAW) 2112/18 to make two Camel claims. In August he was apparently injured in a crash and spent four weeks in hospital. Returning in September, Thöne flew until the Armistice. By his own account, on 11 November he was the last German pilot to fly out of the Bruges area. Post-war, Thöne also served in the *Freikorps*, fighting in Berlin and in the Baltic. As a member of the security police during the Ruhr uprising, he was captured by the Socialists but released. Thöne studied coal mine engineering and was director of a trade organisation before joining the Luftwaffe around 1937. Rising to the rank of colonel, he was captured by British troops at the end of World War 2. Thöne died on 17 January 1974.

Bertram Heinrich scored nine (or ten) victories with MFJ I, mostly in 1917, but his last kill at least was probably in a D VII. He was promoted to Leutnant der Reserve der Matrosenartillerie (MA-naval artillerie) on 18 August 1918 and was killed in action on 31 August 1918 flying a Fokker. His opponent was almost certainly Lt W S Jenkins of No 210 Sqn, Heinrich being the fourth of an eventual 12 victory claims.

MFJ II

Theodor Osterkamp was MFJ II's leading light. A Rhinelander born in Aschersleben on 15 April 1892, he was hoping to go into forestry before the war but joined the Naval Flying Corps instead. In February 1915 Osterkamp underwent observer training at Johannisthal, after which he saw his first service as an observer. On 13 July 1916 he was promoted to reserve officer rank as a Leutnant der Reserve der Matrosenartillerie. 'Theo' claimed his first kill as an LVG observer in *Marine* F. FL. Abt. I on 6 September 1916, downing a Farman. In March 1917 he became a pilot and was assigned to MFJ I, where he had gained six victories by late September. Osterkamp was awarded the 'Hohenzollern' on 20 August – the same day as Sachsenberg.

'Theo' assumed command of MFJ II in March 1918, and by war's end he had achieved at least 28 confirmed victories. He later claimed to have scored 32 kills, but there are few official records about the last three – one historian credits him with 31 victories. Osterkamp held temporary command of the *Marine Jagdgruppe* when Sachsenberg was on leave in September, and received the *Pour le Mérite* on the 2nd of the month. He was subsequently photographed posing with a Fokker E V, but he probably did not fly it operationally. However, Osterkamp's post-war accounts state that his E V was jumped by three SPADs and he was forced to bale out. Despite his own claims, he was certainly flying a D VII in this incident.

Osterkamp's aircraft was marked with vertical black and yellow stripes on the fuselage. In post-war German accounts, it is also reported that he destroyed a British tank on 2 October along with his aircraft victories on this date.

In the 1930s he joined the Luftwaffe and continued to be associated with fighters, commanding JG 51 at the start of World War 2. Osterkamp even flew Bf 109s in combat, adding six more victories to his tally in 1940 and duly winning the Knight's Cross of the Iron Cross. Known as 'Uncle Theo' to his younger subordinates, he rose to the rank of generalleutnant but had to retire at the end of 1944 because of his outspoken views about the High Command. He died in January 1975.

Theo Osterkamp was MFJ II CO when this photograph of Fokker E V 156/18 was taken. He did little, if any, combat flying in this machine, however. It arrived with the unit on 11 August and all Fokker monoplanes were grounded about nine days later due to wing failures. There is no doubt that Osterkamp was a highly-skilled D VII pilot, with at least 28 victories to his credit

Two other MFJ II aces were Vzflgmstr Zenses and Scharon. Alexander Zenses gained 18 victories between June and October 1918, mostly on the D VII. Indeed, he was flying D VII (Alb) 610/18 on 1 August when he was wounded by No 210 Sqn's Lt A L Jones, but returned to action in September. Karl Scharon was credited with at least six confirmed victories between 20 September and 27 October 1918 – he made two more claims on 7 October but these may not have been confirmed.

MFJ III

Marine Feld Jasta III was formed in June 1918 and was certainly equipped with Fokkers in the war's final months. Its CO was Ltn d R MA Gustav Brockhoff, who had claimed his first victory in a Fokker Eindecker in 1916. Brockhoff is known to have flown D VII 4261/18, marked with lengthwise yellow and black stripes on the fuselage. He had at least four confirmed victories.

Vzflgmstr Hans Goerth gained his first two victories in June 1918 flying Albatros D Va 7167/18. On 16 July he shot down a DH 4 flown by No 202 Sqn pilot Lt L A Ashfield DFC, who had survived more than 20 air

Vzflgmstr Franz Mayer (right) of MFJ III scored a victory in this D VII (OAW) 4499/18 on 5 September 1918. The Fokker's fuselage displays white and black diagonal striping, as well as the usual yellow cowling, wheel covers and tail associated with the *Marine* units. The three black stripes on the elevator (not visible in this photograph), which were recorded as identifying MFJ III aircraft on 26 October, may have already been in effect by this time *(A Imrie via HAC/UTD)*

A very well turned out Hans Goerth of MFJ III poses with a Fokker E V painted in unit and personal markings. The cowling, wheels and tail are certainly yellow, with a yellow or white '3'. E V 144/18 and 155/18 arrived on 10 August 1918, but again very little flying was probably done on these machines. Goerth flew D VIIs with success and achieved seven victories by war's end *(P M Grosz)*

battles and shared in five victories with various observers.

On 30 August Goerth downed a Camel from No 65 Sqn in Fokker D VII (Alb) 838/18 – all his remaining victories were scored in D VIIs. His final two kills (his sixth and seventh) took the form of a DH 9 and a Camel downed on 1 October when he was flying a Fokker marked with a black heart on a white band. Another MFJ III D VII ace was Flugmaat Eduard Blaas, who added four to his single March 1918 kill with MFJ II. His final two victories were also a DH 9 and Camel on 1 October, gained flying D VII (OAW) 6381/18 marked with the usual yellow cowling and tail, with a white band around the fuselage.

MFJ IV

Marine Feld Jasta IV was formed in September 1918 from *Staffel* I of the *Seefrosta*. Its most notable pilot was Ltn der MI Reinhold Poss, who had received his commission while still a naval infantryman in June 1915. He joined the naval air service in June 1917. After service in several different units, Poss transferred to MFJ II in February 1918 and then to the *Seefrosta* on 27 April. He had started scoring in May, and had brought his total to five on 16 July, by which time he was probably flying a D VII. Six more victories brought Poss' total to 11, but on 15 October he was brought down and captured. He died in a flying accident on 25 August 1933 when he hit a church steeple at Hagenow.

By the time Gerhard Hubrich joined the unit he already had three kills to his name, scored as a member of the *Seefrosta* in early 1918. Nicknamed *Küken* ('Chick'), he had added eight more by 4 November – the day he downed two Camels in a huge fight with Nos 65 and 204 Sqns. After the war Hubrich found employment as a test and airline pilot before joining the Luftwaffe in 1932, again as a test pilot with the rank of major. Some sources indicate that he added two more victories in World War 2. He died in October 1972. Another MFJ IV ace was FlgMt Albin Buhl, who had three victories with the *Seefrosta* and three more with MFJ IV.

MFJ V

MFJ V was commanded by Ltn z S Eberhard Cranz, and its three most successful pilots were Paul Achilles and Flugmaats Karl Engelfried and Karl Kutschke. Achilles ended the war with at least five confirmed victories and one 'forced to land'. Engelfried had gained one victory in the *Seefrosta* and added four more with MFJ IV. Kutschke had one unconfirmed claim in the *Seefrosta* and three confirmed *Luftsiege* with MFJ V.

MFJ V CO Ltn zur See Eberhard Cranz (right, with flying helmet) seems to have survived a rough landing in his D VII (OAW) with aplomb. The officer at the extreme right inspecting his friend's handiwork is Ltn Paul Achilles, who ended the war with at least five victories. The D VII possibly displays a black and white quartering as a personal emblem and probably the yellow naval unit markings. Note the pale rib tapes on the four-colour fabric-covered wing
(A Imrie via HAC/UTD)

6th ARMY – *JAGDGRUPPE Nr 3*

Jagdgruppe Nr 3 comprised *Jastas* 14, 29, 30, 43, 52 and 63 in the 6th Army from 19 August to 30 September. From then until war's end, it transferred to 4th Army with *Jastas* 14, 16b, 29 and 56. The *Gruppe* was commanded by Oblt Richard Flashar, a former KG 2 pilot and leader of *Jasta* 5 until May 1918, at which time he became JGr CO. In late September Harald Auffarth of *Jasta* 29 took over.

Jasta 14

Ltn Johannes Werner led *Jasta* 14 from September 1917 and, while it is known that the unit flew Albatros scouts and Fokker Triplanes, details of its D VIIs are not available. Some were taken on strength but it is difficult to be certain which pilots achieved victories with them. Vzfw Paul Rothe became an ace in October 1918 after more than a year with the unit but few details survive. It is, however, known that his last two victories were over balloons on 29 October.

Jasta 29

Harald Auffarth led *Jasta* 29 from November 1917, and he would do so until appointed CO of JGr Nr 3 in late September 1918. The unit began to take delivery of D VIIs in July 1918, Auffarth often flying aircraft 387/18 with a *Komet* motif. Perhaps the last 14 of his 29 victories were gained while in a Fokker, Auffarth claiming a DH 9 bomber from No 206 Sqn on 5 October. Its pilot was Lt Clayton Knight, an American who later became famous as an aviation artist. Auffarth's brief combat report stated;

'On 5 October 1918, I shot down a DH 9 (D560 of No 206 Sqn) out

D VII 387/18 was the personal mount of Harald Auffarth, leader of *Jasta* 29 and also of *Jagdgruppe Nr 3*. He scored several victories during October 1918 while flying this machine. Records of his final claims are fragmentary, but the *Heeresbericht* for 30 October confirm his 29th and 30th victories. This D VII displays a green fuselage and yellow nose, with a white comet personal badge. Another early-production Fokker with a Mercedes D IIIa engine, it was tested and accepted on 14 May 1918

of a formation of ten aircraft and forced it to land near Aelbeeke, Belgium. Machine destroyed, pilot wounded, observer uninjured.'

However, fire from the observer Lt J H Perring hit the attacking Fokker, forcing the German ace to land, although the damage was only superficial and he was back in action in 387/18 soon afterwards. Auffarth was recommended for the *Pour le Mérite* after his 20th victory, but it was not approved before the Armistice. After the war he ran a flying school in Münster and died in October 1946.

Jasta 29 produced two other Fokker aces. Uffz Siegfried Westphal joined the unit in late July 1918, and his second victory was over one-legged No 74 Sqn ace Capt S Carlin MC DFC, who was brought down and captured. Westphal's final tally was six kills, four of which were SE 5s. Ltn d R August Burkard was the unit's other ace, and he was also an early summer 1918 arrival. By war's end he too had made six victory claims.

Jasta 30

Jasta 30's CO, Ltn Hans-Georg von der Marwitz, was already an eight-victory ace with the unit by the time the first D VIIs started arriving in July 1918. Born in Ohlau, Silesia, in August 1893, he was the son of General der Kavallerie Georg von der Marwitz, commander of the 2nd Army. Hans-Georg initially served in an Uhlan regiment until transferring to aviation in 1916. Flying with KG 5 and then *Schusta* 10, he gained one victory with the latter unit, then went on to fighters.

Through the hectic days of late 1918 the unit experienced the usual problems of insufficient fuel supplies and inadequate replacement machines. For a period in mid-August, the *Jasta* was 'out of machines and unable to fly', according to Josef Raesch of *Jasta* 43.

Von der Marwitz took his score to 14 or 15 by war's end, winning the 'Hohenzollern'. He was killed in a flying accident on 12 May 1925.

Jasta 43

Eight Fokker D VIIs were on the strength of *Jagdstaffel* 43 by 26 June, but only about two dozen victories were scored by the unit in the last months of the war. CO Adolf Gutknecht, Josef Raesch and Ernst Wiehle were its prominent pilots, ranking ace Oblt Gutknecht flying D VII (Alb) 571/18. Born in September 1891 in Badingen, he had been an army cadet pre-war, and subsequently seen action in France, Bulgaria and Macedonia. Gutknecht then chose to become an observer, before training as a pilot. He had scored a single aerial victory prior to taking over *Jasta* 43 in June 1918.

According to Josef Raesch's diary, Gutknecht was initially a less than effective combat leader, the future ace going through a 'learning curve'. Gutknecht had claimed eight confirmed victories by the end of the war, which ended early

Jasta 43 leader Oblt Adolf Gutknecht and his mechanics are seen with Albatros-built D VII 571/18. It displays a black '1' on the white fin as part of the *Staffel* numbering system. Forward of the white tail unit (*Jasta* 43's marking), the Fokker is decorated in black and white, with a stripe in the same colours just visible on the top wing centre section. In the background is Raesch's D VII ('2' on the fin), marked with a three-pronged pitchfork. Gutknecht was a courageous but inexperienced *Staffel* commander who had his share of leadership difficulties, and as late as 2 September Raesch's diary recorded, 'Tension exists in our *Jasta* with regard to Oblt Gutknecht'. Nonetheless, he attained eight confirmed victories before leaving the *Staffel* due to illness *(Wouter Warmoes collection)*

for him on 25 October when a pulmonary illness saw him hospitalised. Five of his D VII victories were SE 5s and two DH 9 bombers.

Vzfw Ernst Wiehle a native of Harzgerode, experienced his first aerial action with a *Schutzstaffel* in 1917. Born in December 1894, he served in the artillery before moving into aviation in 1916 – Wiehle gained his initial kill in *Schusta* 3 on 6 April 1917. Towards the end of June 1918 he transferred to *Jasta* 43, just as the first D VIIs arrived. Wiehle ended the war with six kills, five of these (all RAF fighters) having been claimed with the D VII.

Ltn Josef Raesch was another successful *Jasta* 43 D VII pilot, although there is disagreement over how many officially-confirmed victories he scored. Raesch was born in Zewen, near Trier, in June 1897. Serving with the infantry until December 1917, he was a late starter. He flew two-seaters with Fl. Abt. 7 before going to *Jasta* 43 in June 1918. Of his early days there he confided to his diary;

'6 June – Took the train to Valenciennes and later on to Lille. I then went to Haubourdin, where *Jasta* 43 is located. The equipment consists mainly of Fokker D VIIs, but the newer pilots are assigned Albatros D IIIs and D Vs.

'10 June – While flying an Albatros D V I met Oblt Gutknecht, who was unsuccessful in trying to pin himself onto my tail. His machine, a Fokker D VII, has a much better rate of climb, but when Gutknecht started to get the upper hand, I spun in and taxied towards the shed. I was told a Fokker D VII was being readied for me.

26 June – Ltn Schmidt got the eighth Fokker D VII to be issued to our *Jasta*, but unfortunately none of them are equipped with the high-compression Mercedes or BMW engines. Consequently, we lose many opportunities during the course of combat because of our low-powered engines (the *Jasta* did later obtain some high-compression Fokkers).

On 29 October 1918 Josef Raesch of *Jasta* 43 wrote, 'At 1645 hrs we took off with *Jastas* 28, 33 and 63. We were soon in the fight we were looking for. Wiehle shot down his first opponent (of the combat). I congratulated Wiehle, who is a dashing pilot'. Here, the 'dashing' Ernst Wiehle (six victories) poses with his Albatros-built DVII, which displays an unknown personal colour from nose to the unit's white tail colouring. Supplementary rib taping has apparently been applied to the centre section of the top wing and a portion of the lower wing *(W Warmoes collection)*

Josef Raesch is seen in the cockpit of the D VII ('2' on the fin, not visible in this photograph) which he inherited from former *Jasta* 43 CO Otto Creutzmann, whose personal fuselage emblem was a three-pronged pitchfork. It seems Creutzmann came from a farming family, as did Raesch. The latter was shot down in this aircraft on 25 July 1918, Raesch being forced to bale out of the flaming D VII. Although he was shocked to see a two-metre hole in his parachute, it still brought him safely down to earth with nothing worse than a badly blistered face. The 'chute was repaired and later saved the life of fellow *Jasta* 43 pilot Ltn Schmidt *(HAC/UTD)*

Although he was no ace, Ltn d R Simons of *Jasta* 43 displays considerable panache in this pose, and in the splendid decoration of his D VII (Alb). This photograph was taken at the *Staffel* airfield at Haubourdin, near Lille, on 26 June 1918. Simons' Fokker displays the unit numeral '3' on the fin, and he would soon have the fuselage sides beneath the tailplane painted white to conform to unit marking practice. Note the way the cross on the underside of the lower wing has been altered, which was a common feature of most *Jasta* 43 Fokkers *(W Warmoes collection)*

'27 June – We took off with *Jasta* 14 at 1030 hrs, and when we arrived at an altitude of 4300 m we noted that our flak units were firing away at a squadron of English fighter 'planes. The Englishmen started to circle, and as soon as I had one in my sights I opened up with a volley from both guns, whereupon the SE 5 went into a vertical climb and then slipped off into a spin, with me closely on his tail. I let him have a second burst, and I could see my tracers entering his cockpit and engine and finally had to pull away to avoid a collision. I spotted my victim some 300 m below me, and saw that the other machines were milling about overhead in a free-for-all. I dived and again opened up with both guns. The SE 5 went into a climb, and now I could see the machine was on fire. The machine spun towards the earth in a tower of fire and finally crashed. I had followed the SE 5 until it hit the ground, and noted that the wreckage was soon surrounded by many of our soldiers who waved to me in a friendly manner. I then flew on home and reported this, my first victory.'

The hot summer weather of 1918 posed a serious problem for the D VII as its phosphorus ammunition was blighted by auto-ignition. This disastrous occurrence cost several pilots their lives. Raesch recalled this and other difficulties facing the *Jagdstaffeln* in the latter half of 1918;

'16 July – Returning to our airfield, we could see the completely burned machine of Wernicke lying in the middle of the field. Our fire fighters were still at work but Wernicke was dead. The hot, oppressive weather had caused the self-ignition of the phosphorus ammunition, and the exploding bullets penetrated the fuel tank and set the machine blazing. He attempted a landing but must have lost his nerve and landed much too hastily, thereby causing the machine to "pancake". We have just heard that a pilot from *Jasta* 29 lost his life in a similar incident.

'20 July – Our fuel provisions are now extremely low and are being rationed. Our motors are more susceptible to malfunctioning. Our ammunition is no longer made from brass but from iron, and substitute material is being used in our fuel lines. We understand that wooden wheels will be substituted for our rubber tyres in the near future. While there is a good supply of flight personnel, they lack combat experience. Despite his great courage, Oblt Gutknecht has only a few air victories and lacks the experience of demonstrating to us how to be masterful when we contact the enemy. I like to fly with him. He calls me a *filzlous* (crab louse) because I stay close to him in all combats.'

On 26 July Raesch saved his life by using a parachute, as he recorded;

'Suddenly a flight of five SE 5s jumped us and we began evasive action. I noticed Blumensaath's and Keller's aircraft were under fire by four of the SEs. Schöbinger was nowhere in sight, and only Gutknecht and I were together. I glanced over my shoulder, then kicked rudder and stick to my left as there was an Englishman on my tail. My manoeuvre led me into the sphere of his deflection shots because Buckingham ammunition passed by my head, entering into my machine. Now my machine was burning. A blazing fire hit my face. I couldn't see anything because of the smoke and flames and I felt my flight boots beginning to shrink.

'I had a feeling that I was lost and immediately my parachute came to mind. I have carried one for the past 14 days and, having the will to live, I looked for the release pin but couldn't find it in the excitement. At last I had it and pulled it out. Then I dropped over the side hoping I wouldn't hit the tail plane. Pulling off my goggles, I saw for the first time that my 'chute hadn't opened. The container that is normally fastened within the 'plane still surrounded all of the shrouds, and only a portion of the silk 'chute had been pulled out.

'I fell like a stone. Fighting for my life, I reached behind me and started stripping the parachute out of the container, when it popped into a full canopy with the sound of a cannon shot. With a jerk the shrouds pulled tight. I floated slowly down to earth. My burning D VII curved above me and then fell away into oblivion.'

Raesch had been shot down by Lt I F Hind of No 40 Sqn for his seventh victory. The German's face was badly blistered, but he was otherwise unharmed. For a time he flew a disappointing Pfalz D XII as a replacement for his D VII but eventually got another Fokker. After

Albatros-built Fokkers of *Jasta* 43 show off their white tail units and gaudy personal markings at Haubourdin on 30 June 1918. Some are ex-*Jasta* 18 machines, which display remnants of that unit's red and white paint scheme. From right to left, they are Uffz Rüggeberg's black-fuselaged D VII, Vzfw Kiep's No '6', with a white star, Ltn Keller's red and white No '4', Ltn Simons' striped No '3', with a fully white tail section, Ltn Wernicke's No '5', with a black chevron, and Raesch's No '2' *(HAC/UTD)*

Gutknecht left, Raesch led the *Staffel* in the air, while Ltn Schobinger was the official acting CO. Raesch's actual victory tally is in some dispute as he is variously credited with three, four or as many as seven victories.

Jasta 52

Paul Billik was the 'star' of *Jasta* 52, his record and achievements putting him head and shoulders above its other pilots. In many ways this was how a number of *Jastas* operated – a superb leader and excellent shot scoring the victories while being protected by his men, with others occasionally managing to pick off the odd aircraft. Of course, if this was achieving results then it was a reasonable tactic and, apparently, one employed by several *jastas*.

It should also be borne in mind that compared to an Allied squadron, which had three flights and some 18 pilots, a German *jasta* was only about the size of a flight. The usual strength of a *Jagdstaffel* was 14 aircraft and 12 to 14 pilots. Many *Amerika Programme Jastas* were under-strength in the high-attrition days of late 1918, some having only eight to ten pilots or even less.

Born in Haatsch, Silesia, Paul Billik joined the air service in May 1916. His first unit in January 1917 was *Schusta* 4, but in March he moved to *Jasta* 12, where he scored four victories before moving to *Jasta* 7 in July. Having eight claims by the end of the year, Billik was appointed CO of the new *Jasta* 52 on 9 January 1918. Most of his pilots were fresh from *Jastaschule Nr* 1, although he had also brought with him four *Jasta* 7 pilots, which was common practice with newly-formed units. Another pattern is evident in the colour scheme Billik selected for the aircraft of his new command – an all-black fuselage, similar to the scheme of his old *Jasta* 7.

Billik was the first to score. On 9 March he shot down two SE 5s, and by month-end he had also destroyed three Camels. By the beginning of August his personal score stood at 31 (23 with his own *Jasta* 52), but on 10 August he was brought down over the front and taken prisoner. His incarceration meant that Billik was excluded from winning the *Pour le Mérite* despite his many victories, all of which had been scored on the British front.

It is not certain who brought him down, for it was the third day of the Battle of Amiens, and aerial engagements were even more confused over a battle zone. At around the time and location that Billik was downed, No 32 Sqn was in combat with D VIIs, and its pilots did claim two 'out of control'. Whether or not one was Billik is not confirmed. He was killed in a flying accident in March 1926.

Jasta 63

In February 1918 Ltn Herman Leptien arrived from *Jasta* 21 to take command of *Jasta* 63. He subsequently scored four times, taking his overall tally to seven. Leptien may have earned his final two or three victories in the D VII. Likewise, Lt Martin Johns gained five of his tally of seven in the summer and autumn of 1918.

AGAINST THE RAF

The 17th Army sector followed the trench lines south into northern France and was adjacent to that of the 6th Army, which, broadly speaking, stretched from the region opposite Arras to Cambrai. South of the 17th was the 2nd Army in the sector around Péronne, while further south still, in the St Quentin area, was the 18th.

In the latter half of 1918, these armies' *jagdstaffeln* would primarily be opposed by the skilled, aggressive and numerous squadrons of the RAF. German airmen greatly respected the efficiency and 'sporting' daring of the British pilots, as Josef Raesch of *Jasta* 43 bluntly noted in his diary entry of 2 September 1918;

'The British are superior to us, not only in number, but in their tactics and organisation'.

Jagdgruppe Nr 8, under 17th Army control, was commanded by Hptm Eduard von Schleich. The 35-victory Bavarian ace had, by then, become popularly known as the 'Black Knight' because he flew black-painted aircraft. Perhaps his final six victories as *Gruppe* leader were scored in the D VII.

JGr 8 was largely comprised of Bavarian units – *Jagstaffeln* 23b, 32b, 35b and Prussian *Jasta* 59 from March to early August 1918. At that point *Jasta* 59 was transferred to JGr 10, leaving JGr 8 with its three Bavarian units. As noted in *Osprey Aircraft of the Aces 53 - Fokker D VII Aces of World War 1 Part 1,* in early October *Jagdstaffeln* 23b, 32b, 34b and 35b were permanently combined to make up Royal Bavarian *Jagdgeschwader* IV. Also under Schleich's command, this short-lived unit survived for about a month before the Armistice came into effect.

Since most of the D VII aces from *Jastas* 23b, 32b, 34b and 35b were covered in the previous volume, the authors will devote little space to profiling the men or their aircraft here, although some brief summaries are in order.

Jasta 23b was led by Ltn Heinrich Seywald, a 24-year-old from Regensburg. A former infantryman, he had achieved two or three victories before the D VIIs arrived and ended the war with six claims. It is uncertain if *Jasta* 23b ever had a full complement of D VIIs, but some of their Fokkers were among the seven machines destroyed by an Allied bombing raid on the unit's Epinoy airfield on 1 August 1918. Seywald and Uffz Michael Hütterer scored the majority of *Staffel* 23b's victories in late 1918.

Jasta 32b only scored a handful of victories in the last months of the war – just five between August and November. One of these was claimed by the CO, Ltn Emil Koch, on 29 August for his seventh victory.

Jasta 34b was led by Oblt Robert Greim, who claimed possibly 13 of his 28 victories in the D VII.

Ltn Rudolf Stark commanded *Jasta* 35b in the last months of the war, and although his actual score is disputed, he may have achieved as many as ten or eleven all told – the last four with D VII (OAW) 4523/18 – plus possibly two more unconfirmed. *Jasta* 35b received six new D VIIs on 24 August.

Hans Helmut von Boddien, wearing his distinctive curassier's cap, is pictured here with a Fokker Dr I during his *Jasta* 11 service. He scored no victories with that famed unit, but would gain five while leading *Jasta* 59 in the summer of 1918. On 27 September his *Staffel* attacked a formation of DH 9s, and their escorting SE 5s, and von Boddien was wounded in the right shin, ending his war *(HAC/UTD)*

This shot was previously published in *Osprey Aircraft of the Aces 53* (on page 77), in which it was erroneously captioned as depicting *Jasta* Boelcke at Aniche. New information indicates that these machines were actually photographed at the airfield at Emerchicourt-Nord in June 1918, with the church tower of Aniche seen in the distance at left. It is quite likely that these are, in fact, 17th Army *Jasta* 59 D VIIs, and that the aircraft at the extreme left (marked 'B') is the personal machine of *Staffelführer* von Boddien. According to respected historian Manfred Thiemeyer, this machine may have had a white nose and tail as well as the white 'B' on a dark band

On 1 August a bombing and strafing raid on the airfield used by *Jastas* 23b and 35b caused serious damage to their equipment Stark wrote that;

'Eleven machines were total write-offs, and all the others except three were badly damaged. The only machines destroyed (in *Jasta* 35b) were the old ones.'

This meant several days of limited activity, and when the Battle of Amiens started on 8 August JGr 8 was still low on aircraft. Stark records one mission in which he led seven aircraft of his *Jasta*, along with nine from 23b and seven from 32b – a total 23 from three *staffeln*. He also noted that *Jasta* 35b was given some Pfalz D XIIs on 1 September. The pilots were not happy, but at least the D XIIs were better than the old Pfalz D IIIa and Albatros machines they had previously flown.

Jasta 59

Oblt Hans-Helmut von Boddien commanded *Jasta* 59 in June 1918 when the unit probably acquired some D VIIs. He was also its main scorer. From Mecklenburg, von Boddien was commissioned in a curassier regiment in 1912. Once the war started, he was seconded to *Reserve Ulanen-Regiment Nr* 2 and was wounded by a trooper's lance in a cavalry clash. Having experienced that age-old style of warfare, he transferred to the new air arm in December 1915. Joining F. Fl. Abt. 18, he flew as observer for pilot Friedrich-Wilhelm Lübbert.

After training as a pilot, von Boddien would follow Lübbert to the famed *Jasta* 11 under von Richthofen in late May 1917 – he seems to have served as both a pilot and an administrative officer. Still without a single victory, von Boddien was appointed CO of *Jasta* 59 at the end of January 1918 and he opened his account on 23 March.

Von Boddien would take his score to five flying the D VII, with two kills in August and a double on 24 September. Three days later he was wounded in the right shin during a fight with SE 5s escorting DH 9s, and he spent three months in hospital.

After the war von Boddien went to Lithuania to fight the Russian Red Army with the *Freikorps* formation Fl. Abt. 424. He disappeared during a flight on 29 November 1919.

Jasta 28w

Württemberg *Jasta* 28 was the top-scoring unit in the 17th Army's *Jagdgruppe Nr 7*, which comprised *Jastas* 28, 33, 57 and 58 from July to mid-October 1918. Ltn Emil Thuy commanded both *Staffel* 28 and the *Gruppe*, the former since the end of October 1917.

Born in Hagen, Westphalia in March 1894, Thuy had been with the army in France until he was wounded in October 1914. Unfit for further service in the field, he became a pilot instead, passing through the usual two-seater route before joining *Jasta* 21 at the beginning of 1917. By the time he moved to *Jasta* 28, he had scored 15 kills.

Thuy had taken his tally to 21 by the time the first D VIIs probably began to arrive with *Jasta* 28 in June 1918. This was the same month in which he received the *Pour le Mérite*. Between then and mid-October Thuy's score rose to 35. Post-war, he

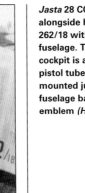

was killed in a flying accident near Smolensk, in the Soviet Union, on 11 June 1930 while training pilots for the newly-formed Luftwaffe.

Jasta 33

Jagdstaffel 33 acquired D VIIs in the summer of 1918, its machines being marked with yellow noses. The unit's leader by mid-July was Carl-August

Jasta 28 CO Lt d R Emil Thuy stands alongside his early Fokker-built D VII 262/18 with its streaky camouflaged fuselage. The fixture beneath the cockpit is a poorly-patched flare pistol tube, with the cartridge rack mounted just below it. The white fuselage band was Thuy's personal emblem *(HAC/UTD)*

This D VII, also in streaked fuselage camouflage, is believed to be a later machine flown by Thuy of *Jasta* 28. It displays a black-outlined white band similar to his previous emblem and later style national insignia. The yellow tailplane with two black stripes was the hallmark of this Württemberg *Staffel*. A leader's streamer trails from the starboard 'N' strut *(HAC/UTD)*

D VII (Alb) 6880/18 was flown by Carl-August von Schönebeck, CO of the yellow-nosed *Jasta* 33. He had learned the trade of the *jagdflieger* under von Richthofen in *Jasta* 11, and assumed his new command after a brief spell with *Jasta* 59. Von Schönebeck brought with him some weighty leadership advice from the 'Red Baron'. 'The leader is the deciding factor for the success of every *Staffel*. Even the best fighter pilots can prove their full worth only if their leader makes proper use of them'. Like the Rittmeister, von Schoenebeck led by example, taking his score to eight with *Jasta* 33 *(Lafayette Foundation)*

von Schönebeck, who was another of von Richthofen's former pilots. Born in Bernstadt, Silesia, in January 1898, he had joined *1 Badisches Leib-Grenadier Regiment Nr* 109 in 1915 at the age of 17. After transferring to the aviation service in December 1916, von Schönebeck briefly flew two-seaters in Fl. Abt. (A) 203, before going to *Jasta* 11 on 7 July 1917. Together with von Boddien, he had claimed three victories by the time he went to *Jasta* 59, with which he added a fourth. Taking command of *Jasta* 33 on 11 July 1918, he doubled his score to become an eight-victory ace, probably flying the D VII for his last four victories.

Late in life, von Schönebeck recalled;

'Our best scout in World War 1 was the Fokker D VII with the BMW engine. I think the SE 5 was the best RFC scout of that war. The British scouts could often turn sharply. The British were more sporting, and we were more military.'

Von Schönebeck, too, remained in close association with flying post-war, serving with the Luftwaffe and rising to the rank of generalmajor. He continued to work in aviation well into his 70s, actually taking up hang-gliding at age 77! He died in September 1989, the last survivor of the Richthofen *Geschwader*.

Vzfw Emil Schäpe was born in Elbin, West Prussia, in October 1890. He served briefly with the infantry in 1912, but in 1915 he began aviation training. Schäpe then flew in two-seaters until his transfer to *Jasta* 5 and later 33. Although his victory tally of 18 is not in doubt, some of his individual kills remain a mystery. Schäpe had made five claims by July 1918, but most came during the hectic days of October. Only actual dates have survived, with no Allied types or locations being recorded. Many of his victories would certainly have been achieved in a D VII.

Jasta 57

Ltn d R Paul Strähle was given command of *Jasta* 57 upon its formation in January 1918, and apart from the period between 27 September and

Jasta 57 pilots pose with their light blue D VIIs at Aniche airfield in September 1918. They are, from left to right, Tracinski (two victories), Hanzog (one), Hechler (two), Jensen (six), CO Paul Strähle (14), Seldner, Blum (three), Wieprich (four), Dudel and Hitschler. The aircraft at the extreme right is Strähle's D VII (OAW) 4025/18, displaying his red nose and fuselage band. Strähle wrote, 'In *Jagdstaffel* 57 we painted the nose of each aircraft in a different colour. All aircraft had the same pale blue fuselages and white rudders, but the different nose colours allowed me to tell at a glance just who was where. After take-off, all my comrades followed me in a staggered line. When I looked along this line, it appeared as a many-coloured palette' *(Peter Kilduff)*

12 October while he recovered from a wound, he led the unit until the war's end.

Strähle was born in May 1893 in Schorndorff, Württemberg. He had been in military service since 1913, having joined *I Kompanie Luftschif-fer-Bataillon Nr 4* as a one-year vol-unteer – he made several pre-war flights in Zeppelin Z VII with the unit. Strähle began pilot training in November 1915, and after service in Fl. Abt. (A) 213, he ended up in *Jasta* 18 in October 1916 and eventually honed his skills as a *jagdflieger* under the stern tutelage of Rudolf Berthold. By the time he was appointed to lead *Jasta* 57 on New Year's Day 1918, Strähle had scored seven kills.

Paul Strähle's OAW-built D VII 4025/18 heads this line-up of *Jasta* 57 Fokkers, all of which display their multi-coloured noses. As the leader's machine, Strähle's was the only one to have a fuselage band in addition to the painted nose *(HAC/UTD)*

D VIIs started to arrive in late July, by which time Strähle had 11 claims. His last four were made while flying his red-nosed pale blue D VII (OAW) 4025/18. He prized the D VII's ability to 'hang on its prop', and wrote that 'with the Fokker we can attack from behind and from below'. However, he had little enthusiasm for massed patrols flown as a *Jagdgruppe*. Such large formations proved difficult to co-ordinate, and he felt the enemy avoided contact with them. He confided to his diary;

'25 August – 1902 hrs to 2010 hrs. We took off together with *Jagdstaffel* 28. The *Jagdgruppe* was rallying above Erchin. Since *Jagdstaffel* 28 was very bad in flying as a unit, I had difficulties in following them. In the region of Haucourt, I attacked an enemy DH 9 squadron which came from Cambrai. Ltn d R Blum shot down a DH 9, which went down vertically and crashed.

'27 August – 0812 hrs to 0920 hrs. *Staffel* reassembled around Hendecourt-Vancourt-St Leger as heavy flak fire greeted us. My Fokker is hit, but not seriously, by a shell fragment. Around Cantin our *Staffel* flies lower to be able to see the higher flying enemy and to avoid being seen by them. Approximately 15 enemy single-seaters are seen near Cherisy. I attack the leading craft, recognise a Fokker, hesitate for a moment but the next 'plane is a Sopwith. I attack from a close distance. Immediately he leaves heavy smoke behind him and I can barely see him – on fire, crashing west of Cherisy (Strähle's 12th confirmed victory). Jensen is attacking a Sopwith Camel, which was sitting on my neck, and he shot it down in the same district.'

Strähle's final two victories came on 29 August, when he led *Jasta* 57 and some other *Staffeln* in a morning attack on an 'armada' of 16 two-seaters and nine No 43 Sqn Camels. He wrote;

'I chased a red *Wimpelmann* (a Camel flying red pennants) and opened fire on him from a close distance. He went down, leaving heavy smoke behind him as he crashed. Immediately I attacked the second Sopwith Camel, who tried to escape by spinning away. Near Cantin he flew very close to the ground, and I thought he was going to land, but then I realised he was continuing to fly just above the tree-tops and rooftops. It developed into a wild chase at 5-10 m height until I placed a shot in his gas tank as he approached our captive balloons. Leaving a heavy smoke trail, he landed south of Brebieres.'

On 27 September Strähle was flying with his own *Staffel* and *Jasta* 28 when they attacked a DH 4 formation. He recorded;

'I got close to one of them and opened fire on him from underneath. Suddenly, I felt a strong hit on my right forehead. I realised immediately that I had been hit by an English bullet and began gliding to our field at Aniche. Because of the heavy bleeding, my glasses were completely dimmed with blood. I landed smoothly and was taken to the first aid car, where I was bandaged and taken at once to the hospital.'

The glancing bullet had hit Strähle on the forehead, effectively ending his combat career. He took French leave from the hospital to return to his unit on 7 October, but a high fever and influenza kept him from flying in the final chaotic weeks. After the war Strähle ran his own automobile company, and in World War 2 saw further service as a major in France, the Low Countries and in Russia. He died in 1985.

Ltn Johannes Jensen scored five of his six victories in a D VII, with another unconfirmed, between April 1918 and the end of the war. He also briefly led *Jasta* 57 while Strähle was recovering from his wound.

Jasta 58

Prussian *Jagdstaffel* 58 probably had D VIIs in July, just as new CO Oblt Hermann Martini arrived. For once the commander was not the leading light of a unit, this distinction falling to Ltn Martin Demisch. Born in Bautzen in November 1896, he had joined the *Jasta* in February 1918. By 18 June he had four victories, and had taken his score to ten by 24 September. On this date Demisch and others were in a fight with No 40 Sqn SE 5as, the former apparently shooting down Capt G J 'Ben' Strange, brother of the famous Col L A Strange DSO MC. During the action, however, another SE 5a shot up his D VII and the badly wounded Demisch was forced to land near Abancourt. He died the next day.

While two No 40 Sqn pilots fired at Fokkers in this fight, the best report came from 2Lt G Stuart Smith in SE 5a E3046. He wrote;

'Whilst flying behind the formation, SE pilot observed a Fokker biplane stalling up to secure a favourable position to attack. SE did a climbing turn to frustrate this and saw another EA stalling up on the right. SE immediately did a half roll to the left and got a full drum of Lewis and 100 rounds of Vickers into the first EA at point blank range. EA went down out of control, spinning and side-slipping with smoke issuing from the cockpit. SE was unable to follow EA down owing to being attacked by two other EA and driven down for about 4000 ft.

'This EA is confirmed on fire by Lt A T Drinkwater of the same patrol.'

Jasta 1

Another 17th Army *Jagdgruppe* was *Nr* 10, which comprised *Jastas* 1, 39 and 59 from mid-August to 26 September 1918, when 39 was dropped. On 17 October *Jastas* 1, 57, 58 and 59 switched to *Jagdgruppe Nr* 4.

It appears that *Jasta* 1 may not have scored many successes with the D VII, despite being led by ex-*Gruppe* CO Rittmeister Kurt von Döring. He was an experienced fighter leader, having commanded *Jasta* 4 and then served as acting CO of *Jagdgeschwader* I when von Richthofen was

37

absent. In February 1918, he became leader of JGr 4, then *Jasta* 1 in September. Von Döring had scored nine victories by the end of 1917, but he added just two more in October 1918, probably in a D VII.

The leading *Jasta* 1 ace by this time was Ltn Raven Freiherr von Barnekow, who had previously flown with Karl Plauth in *Jasta* 20. Von Barnekow was commissioned in the 2nd Guards *Uhlan* Regiment just before his 18th birthday, and following service in a Guards Foot Regiment, he began the career change to fighter pilot. Von Barnekow saw combat under von Döring with *Jasta* 4, *Jasta* 11 and *Jasta* 4 again, then went to *Jasta* 20, where he shot down four British aircraft in the first half of 1918. Upon joining *Jasta* 1, probably flying a D VII, he added three more in September and then a final four in October.

In World War 2 von Barnekow served in the Luftwaffe on the staff of his old CO, now Gen von Döring, and remained close friends with another old comrade, Ernst Udet. Shortly after Udet's suicide in November 1941, von Barnekow also killed himself.

Jasta 39

Jasta 39 gained 41 victories during its service in Italy on the Isonzo Front in 1917, before returning to the Western Front in March 1918. Its leader in the war's final months was Ltn Johann Hesselink, formerly with *Jasta* 33. Unusually, Hesselink was a volunteer from neutral Netherlands, serving in the German Army.

Jasta 39 left JGr 10 in late September to fly defensive sorties against the British Independent Air Force (IAF) while stationed at Bühl in the *Armee Detachment A*.

Vzfw Hans 'Franz' Nülle, born in Gross Heiden in December 1897, had been an apprentice blacksmith pre-war. The conflict in Europe changed that, however, and he transferred to the aviation service and served in two-seaters in Fl. Abt. 72 in 1916, then bombers, before finally becoming a fighter pilot. Nülle joined *Jasta* 39 in April 1918, but did not score a victory until 1 September. By war's end he had accumulated a total of 11 kills, which included four balloons shot down on the evening of 15 September and two DH 9 bombers of No 104 Sqn IAF on 6 November.

Ltn Wilhelm Sommer came to *Jasta* 39 in July 1918 and scored five victories, including two balloons, by the end of September. Reinhold Jörke was another ace. An able NCO pilot who scored ten kills with *Jastas* 12 and 13 before joining *Jasta* 39 in June 1918, his last four victories may all have been scored with a D VII.

────── 2nd ARMY – JAGDGRUPPE Nr 2 ──────

Jagdstaffeln 5 and 46 comprised *Jagdgruppe Nr 2* from June to 8 August 1918. *Jastas* 34b and 37 were added to its establishment in early October, although on the 7th *Jasta* 34b became part of Bavarian JG IV. This *Gruppe* therefore finished the war with the remaining three *staffeln* (5, 37 and 46). The group's CO was Oblt Richard Flashar, who had taken over in March 1918. A long-serving pilot and regular army officer, Flashar had commanded *Jasta* 5 from July 1917. When *Jagdgruppe Nr 2* was reorganised in August, Oblt d R Otto Schmidt became leader until war's end, having also taken command of *Jasta* 5.

Jasta 5 CO Otto Schmidt (left) poses with Ltn d R Otto Könnecke who wears his newly-awarded *Pour le Mérite*, dating the photograph as being post-26 September 1918. Könnecke's victory tally was at least 32 by this time, and he would finish the war with 35 kills. Schmidt would claim at least 20 aircraft and be recommended for the 'Blue Max', but he missed out on the award due to the Armistice. *Jasta* 5 was sometimes called the *Kanonenstaffel* (aces' squadron), being the third highest scoring *Jasta* with over 250 victories *(J Ladek)*

Fritz Rumey was the most successful *Jasta* 5 ace with 45 victories. Like Könnecke, he would earn a commission in the reserves and the *Pour le Mérite*. However, he would not survive the war, being killed on 27 September 1918 – the day he scored his 44th and 45th victories. Dogfighting with SE 5as of No 32 Sqn, Rumey took to his parachute but the canopy failed to deploy *(Franks collection)*

The best-known example of a *Jasta 5* Fokker is zebra-striped D VII (OAW) 4598/18, which was used by ace Josef Mai to score two of his thirty victories. It is said that this machine was previously used by fellow ace Otto Könnecke. The black and white striping may have been intended to disrupt the aim of enemy airmen

Jasta 5

By replacing its Dr I Triplanes with D VIIs in late June, *Jasta* 5 may have had a full complement of the new Fokker fighters by August. It used the machines to good effect, finishing the war as the third-highest scoring *staffel* with over 250 kills – a tally exceeded only by *Jastas* 11 and 2 Boelcke.

Otto Schmidt was born in Neukirchen-Saar in March 1885, and he entered military service early, becoming a Hussar officer in 1910. When war came he was serving with *Jäger Regiment zu Pferde Nr 12*, and he remained infantryman until he was wounded in March 1915. Transferring as an oberleutnant to the aviation service in 1916, Schmidt first flew as an observer, and was credited with two victories, before becoming a fighter pilot. Transferring to *Jasta* 7, he added two more kills to his tally and then three more with *Jasta* 32, which he commanded.

Finally, Schmidt moved to *Jasta* 29 as *Staffelführer*, and his overall score had risen to ten by the end of September 1917. Wounded by ground fire during a balloon attack in October, he recovered to take command of *Jasta* 5 on 3 July 1918. His final score was at least 20 (possibly as many as 25), but his final claims, like the recommendation for the *Pour le Mérite*, were not confirmed. Eight of Schmidt's victories were balloons.

Born in 1895, Uffz Karl Treiber joined *Jasta* 5 in September 1918 and gained seven victories in the war's final weeks. The fuselage of Treiber's D VII was marked with a large 'T' on its side. He flew Bf 109 fighters during the Battle of Britain but was shot down and captured on 27 September 1940. Repatriated later in the war almost certainly because of his age, Treiber returned to active service – as an adjutant – with JG 52 in 1945.

Jasta 5, however, was more famous for its three highly successful pilots, Fritz Rumey, Otto Könnecke and Josef Mai. All were NCOs for most of their careers, and since all three won the Golden Military Merit Cross, which was the highest Prussian bravery award for NCOs, they were often called the 'Golden Triumvirate'.

Born in Königsberg in March 1891, Fritz Rumey served with the infantry on the Eastern Front before joining the air service. He first flew as an observer before becoming a pilot, and after a brief stay with *Jasta* 2, he moved to *Jasta* 5 as a vizefeldwebel on 10 June 1917. A balloon represented

his first victory on 6 July 1917, and he had scored four more victories, and was wounded twice, by the end of the year. By 7 June 1918 Rumey's score stood at 23, when he and was finally promoted to Leutnant der Reserve. He probably began flying the D VII soon afterwards, and was reportedly known as the 'yellow Fokker flier', from which it may be assumed that his D VII was largely painted yellow.

In September alone Rumey scored 16 times, including 'triples' on the 16th and 17th, to take his tally to 45 (with about 22 on the D VII) by the 27th – he also had four unconfirmed victories. Rumey received the 'Blue Max' on 10 July, shortly after being commissioned. The top-scoring *Kanone* (ace) of his *Jasta*, Rumey was killed on 27 September whilst dog-fighting with SE 5as of No 32 Sqn.

As with many World War 1 aces, there are conflicting versions of how the great ace met his death. It had long been thought that Rumey's D VII collided with the SE 5a of Lt G Lawson, but others believe he fell to the fire of Lt F L Hale. However, his fellow *Jasta* 5 pilots were convinced that his D VII had suffered a wing failure during a full-throttle dive in pursuit of an SE 5a. What is certain is that Rumey took to his parachute, but it failed to open and he plunged to his death.

Otto Könnecke was born in Strasbourg on 20 September 1892. A carpenter by trade, he joined the army in 1911 and learned to fly in 1913. When war broke out he was an instructor, a he continued to train would-be pilots until late 1916. Posted to Macedonia, Könnecke flew with *Jasta* 25, and scored two victories, before moving to France and *Jasta* 5 in April 1917. During the summer he began to score steadily, ending the year with 11 successes. Könnecke continued to claim more kills in 1918, and his tally had reached 23 by the time the D VII had become more or less established with the unit. Promoted to leutnant on 15 June, he then won the 'Hohenzollern' on 20 July.

Könnecke 35th, and last, victory came on 4 November, one week before the Armistice. By then he had received the *Pour le Mérite* (on 26 September). Post-war, Könnecke flew with Lufthansa, and in 1935 he joined the Luftwaffe and subsequently commanded flying schools as a major. He died in January 1956.

The third member of *Jasta* 5's 'golden triumvirate', Josef Mai, was born on 3 March 1887 and he joined the air service in 1915. He had served in KG 5 prior to becoming a fighter pilot, and he eventually joined *Jasta* 5 in March 1917. Mai took time to become proficient in his new role, and did not score his first victory until 20 August – however, by year's end his tally had risen to five. His 13th victory came on 2 June 1918, and his first success in the D VII – flying 595/18 – took the form of a Camel downed on the 27th. Mai used this same aircraft to gain his next five kills, including a double on 8 August. He was flying D VII (Alb) 898/18 (apparently fitted with a high-compression engine) on 19 August when he enjoyed one of his best days. O'Brien Browne has translated this account;

'I took off at 0735 hrs and led my *Kette* of five aircraft to the Péronne area to deny the approaches of the English observation aircraft, which had been coming out very strongly. When I was over Péronne with my flight, between two cloud layers, I saw two English aircraft flying along the Roman Road in a westward direction. I stepped on the gas and tried to block the Tommies' way. Because I had my fast aircraft, my *Kette* receded

Ltn d R Josef Mai was the third of the 'golden triumvirate' of *Jasta* 5 aces who began their careers as NCO pilots. Like Rumey and Könnecke, he was eventually commissioned, but unlike them he failed to win the *Pour le Mérite*. Seen here with his OAW-built D VII 4598/18, Mai survived the conflict

ever further behind me. I couldn't give any thought to this because the Tommies would have escaped me. We were approaching the front, closer and closer. Already the first English flak was commencing to fire – there was a slim chance that I would come within shooting distance. Then I gunned my crate and laid phosphorus ammunition in front of one of the Tommies' noses. The success was amazing. Hardly were my first shots away when I saw only debris instead of the English aircraft flying into the air. However, the English flak came into action all the stronger.

'The phosphorus trails had caused one aircraft to try to avoid them, and at the same time both aircraft collided. A double victory for me (two No 48 Sqn Bristol F2B Fighters). As my *Kette* caught up to me, the dogfight was already over and we turned our backs to the English flak fire.

'On the return flight, we again flew through the cloud layers. North of Péronne we suddenly came upon an English SE 5 single-seater squadron, which was flying under us. We turned around and dove on to the Tommies, who didn't want to accept battle with us. Instead, they dived for home. I was successful in getting an SE in front of my machine guns, which I shot down with my first burst from both guns. Thus could I shoot down my 21st, 22nd and 23rd opponents in less than two hours.'

Mai continued to score in D VII 898/18, as well as in 564/18 and in his black and white striped (OAW) 4598/18. On 29 September his score reached 30, 15 of which had been claimed with the D VII. Mai was commissioned and nominated for the 'Blue Max', although it had not been approved by war's end. He died in January 1982.

Jasta 37

Ltn d R Georg Meyer was *Jasta* 37's final commander. He arrived from *Jasta* 7 on 14 April with four victories and remained CO to war's end. Born in Bremen in January 1893, he initially saw combat as an infantryman, although he soon transferred to the air service and fought in Macedonia. As a fighter pilot, Meyer moved to France and *Jasta* 22, followed by further service with *Jasta* 37. By the time the first D VIIs arrived at the latter unit, Meyer's score had reached possibly as many as

Jasta 37 leader Ltn d R Georg Meyer is seated in the front row in this picture directly behind the chalked sign, together with his groundcrew. He was apparently about to leave to get married when this photograph was taken, as the sign reads 'farewell to the bachelor's life, 18.9.18'. Meyer did not stay away long, as he was credited with an SE 5a on 20 September. At right is one of the unit's Fokkers, and the wings of a Pfalz D XII can be seen at left

ten. On 8 August – the first day of the Battle of Amiens – he claimed three DH 9 bombers, two of which fell during a morning raid. These aircraft were probably from No 98 Sqn, although unit records indicate that only one bomber was lost. By the end of the war Meyer's score stood at 24, and although nominated for the *Pour le Mérite,* he never received it due to the Armistice. Meyer was killed in a motorcycle accident on 15 September 1926.

Fully kitted out for flight, *Jasta* **37 CO Ltn d R Georg Meyer poses in his flying gear with his groundcrew. His Albatros-built D VII was emblazoned with a black-bordered white diagonal band and probably a black engine cowling. On 8 August 1918 – the opening day of the Battle of Amiens – Meyer downed three aircraft and unsuccessfully attacked a balloon. It may have been the 'black day of the German Army', but it was a successful one for the** *Fliegertruppe,* **which claimed 64 victories**

On the outbreak of war Ltn d R Heinrich Henkel was an artilleryman, although he soon transferred to the infantry and was subsequently wounded in September 1916. Following his recovery, Henkel became an officer in the air aviation service. By May 1918 he had been posted to *Jasta* 37, and most of his eight victories were scored with the D VII. Nicknamed *Heinrich der Hesse,* he had the nose of his Fokker fighter painted in red back to the cockpit as a personal marking.

Ltn d R Fritz Blume, who also served as the *Staffel* adjutant, probably scored at least four victories in a D VII in the last month of the war. His nickname was *gelbe Fritz* (yellow Fritz), so he had the nose of his Fokker painted yellow.

Born in Hamburg, Ltn d R Albert Hets, was just two months older than Heinrich Henkel. He scored six victories with *Jasta* 37 before dying in action on 10 August 1918 while flying D VII (Alb) 712/18 – Hets had scored his final victory earlier that same day. Three or four of his kills were probably scored in a D VII.

Jasta 46

Although Otto Creutzmann was the last wartime CO of *Jasta* 46, his first five victories were claimed with various other units – *Jasta* 20, *Kest* 4b and *Jasta* 43 – before he was given a command. With this unit, he added three more aerial victories, in August 1918, and these were almost certainly scored in a D VII. Creutzmann died in 1943.

The two *Jasta* stars, however, were Vzfw Oskar Hennrich and OfStv Robert Heibert. The former had commenced his flying career as an observer/gunner with KG 2, serving with the unit between April 1916

Eight Fokker D VIIs and one Albatros of *Jasta* **46 sit smartly lined up on Moislains airfield in August-September 1918. Each aircraft's fuselage is painted in the black and white** *Staffel* **colours. On the extreme left is one of 'balloon-busting' ace Oskar Hennrich's machines, marked with his distinctive 'H' emblem** *(A Imrie)*

Robert Heibert was another of *Jasta* 46's NCO aces, and he is seen here showing off his Golden Military Merit Cross – the so-called *Pour le Mérite für Unteroffiziere* (NCOs). He survived the war with 13 victories, and had several more unconfirmed claims

Vzfw Oskar Hennrich stands alongside his D VII marked with his bold 'H' emblem. This is believed to be an Albatros-built D VII, with a BMW engine, but the port lower wing, covered in four-colour fabric, was a replacement from an OAW product. The aircraft is white from the cockpit aft, with a black forward fuselage

Heinrich Kroll was both the CO and top ace of *Jasta* 24, the unit's war diary crediting him with 34 victories, although his generally accepted official tally was 30. As commander of a Saxon unit, he was awarded the Saxon Albert Order, Knight 2nd Class with Swords. He also received the 'Hohenzollern' on 22 February 1918 and the 'Blue Max' on 29 March

and February 1917. Becoming a pilot, Hennrich flew two-seaters until he transferred to fighters with his posting to *Jasta* 46 in early May 1918. He was an ace by the time the D VIIs arrived, and downed his 20th opponent on 1 October, although two of his kills may not have been officially confirmed. Of his victories, 13 were over kite balloons. He appears to have been commissioned in the final weeks of the war.

Robert Heibert was born in Oberfall, in the Mosel region, in January 1886. Joining up in August 1914, he was to be wounded four times before war's end. Joining the air service in May 1915, Heibert flew two-seaters, mostly over Verdun, and on becoming a fighter pilot he served with *Jasta* 33 in 1917. He moved to *Jasta* 46 when it was formed in December, and by the summer of 1918 had nine victories. Heibert's last three or four victories were attained with the D VII, and while his final score reached 13, he also had seven more unconfirmed claims. Heibert died in May 1933 by his own hand.

Dresden-born Ltn Helmut Steinbrecher also became a D VII ace, possibly scoring victories four and five with the Fokker fighter before the Armistice. Another two claims were not upheld, being awarded instead to other pilots. Steinbrecher gained notoriety on 27 June 1918 when he parachuted successfully from his burning Albatros D Va, thus becoming one of the first German fighter pilots to do so.

18th ARMY – *JAGDGRUPPE Nr 12*

Jagdgruppe Nr 12 comprised *Jagdstaffeln* 24, 42, 44 and 79b from April 1918 to war's end. Its first leader was Ltn d R Heinrich Kroll, *Staffelführer* of Saxon *Jasta* 24. Hasso von Wedel took over both commands on 21 August 1918, a week after Kroll had been wounded.

Jasta 24

Heinrich Kroll came from the Flensberg area of Kiel, where he had been born the son of a schoolmaster on 3 November 1894. He was going to follow in his father's footsteps but he enlisted in the army on the outbreak of war. Decorated and commissioned by mid-1915, Kroll transferred to the air service and flew Rumpler two-seaters. Moving to *Jasta* 9 in November 1916, he had scored five kills by May 1917 –

The coat of arms of the von Wedel family was a West Prussian *Richtrad*, the medieval wheel device used for torture and execution. Hasso von Wedel, final *Jasta* 24 CO, applied this red emblem to most of his fighters, including this OAW-built D VII, which he probably flew during his service with the *Staffel*

he had also been appointed CO of *Jasta* 24. By the end of the year Kroll had achieved 15 victories, and he had doubled his tally by mid-1918. His last ten successes were gained as CO of JGr 12 in a D VII, with one of his machines being (Alb) 660/18. Post-war, Kroll went into business, although he commenced flying regularly again in 1928 when he joined the Hamburg Flying Club. The following year Kroll became a commercial pilot, but his new career was cut short when he contracted pneumonia and subsequently died on 21 February 1930.

Hasso von Wedel was an experienced aviator long before he took command of JGr 12 on 21 August 1918. Indeed, he had flown with no fewer than five two-seater units and three *jastas.* Yet despite seeing much action von Wedel scored just five kills, the last three of which were gained while leading *Jasta* 24 and the *Gruppe* in a D VII.

Jasta 24's history records that the first ten D VIIs arrived on 28 May from *Armee Flugpark* 18. The unit in turn handed back six Albatros D Vs and sent two others to *Jasta* 69. Three days later, while flying a D VII, Kroll shot down a Bréguet 14 to record his 24th and the unit's 61st victory.

The other *Kanone* to see service with *Jasta* 24 was Offz Stv Friedrich Altemeier, who came from Niederbecksen, near Hannover. Born in June 1886, he worked in a Krupps factory pre-war and attended military school from 1906 through to 1908. Serving as a machine gunner in the infantry upon the outbreak of war, Altemeier was wounded in January 1915. He then transferred to the air service and, after a period on two-seaters, went to *Jasta* 14 and then *Jasta* 24. Altemeier scored nine victories in 1917 and a further five in the spring of 1918. His own aircraft were often decorated with the Krupps industrial emblem of three intertwined rings.

Wounded in 1917 and again on 25 July 1918, Altemeier was awarded the Silver Wound Badge. He also received the Golden Military Merit Cross. Returning to his unit after the D VIIs' arrival, Altemeier continued to raise his score until war's end. His tally reached 21 kills just 24 hours prior to the Armistice coming into effect, although this final claim probably remained unconfirmed.

The only other *Jasta* ace to fly a D VII was Vzfw Kurt Ungewitter, a pre-war pilot. His first victories – two, plus one forced to land – were achieved as a *Schutzstaffel* pilot. Ungewitter joined *Jasta* 24 on 6 June 1918, and on 18 October he was flying D VII 361/18 when he attacked a balloon. He emerged from the engagement with his aircraft so badly shot up by anti-aircraft fire that he had to force-land behind in German lines, inflicting further damage on his already battered Fokker. The fuselage of 361/18 was duly repaired and given new wings, but twelve days later Ungewitter was again forced down in the same D VII after a fight with SE 5as. This time the Fokker had to go to the *Flug Park* for repair.

By war's end, Ungewitter had taken his tally to seven, the last four with the D VII. He was killed in a flying accident in March 1927.

Jasta 42

Ltn der Landwehr Karl Odebrett was *Jasta* 42's leader, having been its CO since its formation in December 1917. Born in Schneidemühl in July 1890, he had learned to fly in February 1914, and when war broke out he fought on the Eastern Front. In 1917 Odebrett served with *Jasta* 16b in France, and by the time he became *Jasta* 42 CO, he had seven kills – this had been increased to 12 by 4 May 1918. Flying the D VII, Odebrett took his score to 21, although records for his last five victories were lost at war's end. If correct, however, nine of his kills were scored with the Fokker. Odebrett died in Venezuela from kidney failure in February 1930.

Jasta 44s

Uffz Bernard Bartels was a D VII ace in Saxon *Jasta* 44. He, too, had served as a two-seater pilot, in Fl. Abt. (A) 233, and only joined *Jasta* 44 in September 1918. Bartels immediately showed his ability as a fighter pilot by claiming four balloons and a Camel before hostilities ceased.

Paul Lotz joined from *Jasta* 7 in April 1918 with four victories to his credit. Born in Rumenau in October 1895, he had become CO of *Jasta* 44 on 10 June, and scored his fifth victory on 21 July. Lotz's last four kills, together with one unconfirmed, may have been achieved while flying the D VII, lifting his score to nine. Lotz was killed at his aerodrome at Doustiennes on 23 October when his aircraft crashed due to wing failure.

Jasta 79b

By the time *Jasta* 79b received its first D VIIs in August 1918, Ltn d R Hans Böhning had been its CO for six months. Born in Bavaria in July 1893, he had initially served in the artillery before joining the air service and flying two-seaters. Böhning eventually transferred to fighters when he joined *Jasta* 36, and during his time with this unit he claimed four kills – his fifth victory came after his move to *Jasta* 76b. In February 1918 Böhning was appointed CO of *Jasta* 79b, and he ended the war with 17 kills, of which the last five were possibly downed with the D VII. Wounded flying D VII (Alb) 747/18 in combat with DH 9s over Soriel on 20 September, Böhning returned to active duty on 1 November as CO of *Jasta* 32b. He died in a gliding accident on 20 October 1934.

Friedrich Altemeier poses with an early Fokker-built D VII, which is probably not his own. This machine displays the typical 'streaky' camouflage on its fuselage and some form of white marking. It does not display Altemeier's usual symbol, which was the three intertwined rings of the Krupps factory logo. Altemeier was one of the original members of *Jasta* 24, and he spent his entire career as a fighter pilot with the unit

FIGHTING THE FRENCH AND THE AMERICANS

S outh of the German 18th Army near St Quentin, the jagged line of the Western Front angled in a south-easterly direction. Adjacent was the 9th Army, then the 7th, opposite Soissons and Compiégne, with the 1st Army to the south-west. Next in line were the 3rd and 5th, whose lines stretched from Reims (Rheims) west to Verdun and included the Chàteau-Thierry area. Army Group 'C' occupied the region around St Mihiel.

As a result, the *Jasta* pilots attached to these armies, especially in the 5th and Group 'C' armies, were opposed by the French *Aviation Militaire* in the war's final months. They would also encounter the well-equipped, but inexperienced, airmen of the infant United States Air Service.

The French contribution to the Allied aerial effort in 1918 was massive. By late March, the French air service was equal in size to the German aviation establishment, with 2750 aircraft at the front (1350 fighters and 1400 two-seaters) and 580 in reserve. French airmen were equipped with the excellent SPAD VII and XIII fighters, and many bombing *escadrilles* flew the superb Bréguet XIV. By the second half of the year, massed formations of Bréguets regularly raided tactical targets behind German lines. Initially, they were escorted by SPADs and later by the heavily-armed Caudron R XI three-seaters. All were tough opponents for *Jasta* pilots.

7th ARMY – JAGDGRUPPE Nr 4

By around 10 June 1918, *Jagdgruppe Nr* 4 comprised *Jastas* 21, 39, 60 and 81. Two months later *Jasta* 39 was transferred, but the other three units remained with the *gruppe* until mid October. By the time the first D VIIs started to arrive, JGr 4 was led by Oblt Oskar Freiherr von Boenigk, *Staffelführer* of Saxon *Jasta* 21. It was a command he had assumed at the end of October 1917. From June 1918 he began to score heavily against aircraft and balloons. On 11 August von Boenigk's tally had reached 21, and he was awarded the *Pour le Mérite* in October, by which time he had left the unit to take command of JG II. Von Boenigk's final score reached 26.

Oblt Oskar Freiherr von Boenigk was briefly experimenting with a moustache and goatee beard when this photograph of his *Jasta* 21 personnel was taken, circa August 1918. They are, from left to right Uffz Heinrich Haase (half hidden, with five victories), Vzfw Max Kuhn (12), Karl Thom (27), Ltn Josef Seebald, Oblt von Kalkreuth (the OzbV, who was a non-flying officer for special duty), von Boenigk (26), Oblt von Brockel (one), Ltn Julius Keller (two), Ltn Christians (two) and Ltn Hilmar Glöcklen *(HAC/UTD)*

Jasta 21s

An indomitable Prussian, Karl Thom was the star performer of *Jasta* 21. He was born near Freystatt on 18 May 1893, the son of a farm worker, and he entered military service in 1911 with *Husaren-Regiment Nr* 5. By the outbreak of war Thom had been posted to *Jäger Regiment zu Pferde Nr* 10, and after being wounded in November 1914 he transferred to the air service. He flew two-seaters in the Vosges region with Fl. Abt. (A) 216 until he was injured in a crash in May 1916. He then saw duty with F. Fl. Abt. 48 in Rumania, where he was forced down and taken prisoner. Thom made a daring escape and received the Iron Cross 1st Class.

After briefly serving with Fl. Abt. (A) 234, he became a *jagdflieger* with *Jasta* 21 in May 1917, shortly before Eduard Schleich took command of the unit. Thom had scored 14 victories by the end of the year, and been awarded the Golden Military Merit Cross.

During a balloon attack on 23 December, he was again badly wounded, this time in the leg. Back with the *Jasta* on 24 January 1918, Thom continued to fly even though his leg was still healing. His scoring would only pick up as the D VIIs arrived in June, and he had raised his tally to 27 by 11 August, when he was seriously wounded in the hip. Whilst in hospital he was promoted to Leutnant der Reserve. Returning to his unit on 6 November, Thom was greeted with the news that he had won the *Pour le Mérite,* having already been awarded the exclusive Member's Cross with Swords of the Royal Hohenzollern House Order. On 9 November he suffered his final crash, resulting in various broken bones and the ending of his war.

In World War 2 Thom served in the Luftwaffe, and he was eventually reported missing on the Eastern Front and never heard from again.

Ltn d R Fritz Höhn was born in Wiesbaden in May 1896. Another

This splendid view of Karl Thom's D VII (OAW) 2052/18 reveals the *Jasta* 21 pattern of personal and *Staffel* markings. The old unit emblem of a vertical black and white fuselage stripe was considerably wider than that displayed on earlier aircraft. Most of the unit's D VIIs had personal colours applied to noses and tails, and on Thom's machine these elements were probably black. In addition, he displayed his traditional personal badge of an angular black 'T' with thin white border. The white serial number on the aft fuselage is obscured by the black tail marking, but it appears on the wheel covers as *Fok D7 OAW 2052/18* and has also been applied to the undercarriage and forward 'N' strut *(A Imrie)*

Karl Thom poses for posterity with his mechanics. This half-tone photograph is important because it shows the 'T' marking on the upper starboard wing of Thom's OAW-built 2052/18. The letter does not have a white outline on this surface. The personal marking is almost certainly repeated on the port wing in the same position and possibly also beneath each lower wing *(A Imrie)*

former infantryman, he joined *Jasta* 21 around November 1917, and by the time the D VIIs arrived had notched up six victories – two aircraft and four balloons. By the end of the war Höhn had achieved a further 15 kills, including six more balloons, although the details of his October claims are unknown. He had left *Jasta* 21 by then, going first to *Jasta* 81 at the beginning of September and then *Jasta* 60, before finally joining *Jasta* 41. Höhn was killed in action with the latter unit on 3 October 1918.

Uffz Heinrich Haase gained his first acknowledged victory while flying with *Schutzstaffel* 8 in May 1918. Joining *Jasta* 21 after it had switched to D VIIs, he shot down five balloons between 4 August and 10 October, but was wounded on the latter date and saw no further action. Another successful NCO pilot, and balloon specialist, in this unit was Max Kuhn. He destroyed eight 'sausages', plus four aircraft with the D VII. Finally, Ltn d R Paul Turck arrived from *Jasta* 66 in July with a score of five victories, of which possibly one or two were scored with D VIIs. He doubled his score to ten with *Jasta* 21.

Jasta 60

Ltn Arnd (sometimes seen spelled 'Arno') Benzler was leading *Jagdstaffel* 60 when it probably received its first D VIIs in June 1918. He had initially seen combat flying two-seaters in *Artillerie Flieger Abteilung* 207, where he scored his first victory with his observer on 14 December 1916. Benzler then went to *Jasta* 32, then 45, 65 and finally 60, having achieved three more victories along the way. With *Jasta* 60 he took his score to nine. Fritz Höhn was in temporary command while Benzler was on leave in September 1918, during which time Höhn added six kills to his tally.

Günther Dobberke claimed one victory with *Jasta* 45 before moving to *Jasta* 60 as the D VIIs arrived. He had added another seven kills by 15 October, when he was injured in a crash whilst collecting a new D VII from AFP (*Armee Flug Park*) 3. Ltn Arthur Korff scored all eight of his victories (two balloons and six SPADs) as an NCO with the unit in 1918.

A future Fokker ace was Ltn d R Karl Waldemar Ritscherle, who was born in Karlsruhe, Baden, in May 1898. He saw active service on the Eastern Front for two years with 1 *Badisches Leib-Dragoner Regiment Nr* 20, before becoming a gunner with *Schutzstaffel* 8 in April 1917. Ritscherle gained three kills whilst performing this role, the first being over Sgt Andrew Campbell of the Lafayette *Escadrille* on 1 October.

After being promoted to leutnant, Ritscherle spent several months as a gunnery instructor before training as a pilot and being posted to *Jasta* 60 on 22 June 1918. He had scored five more victories before the war ended. In World War 2 Ritscherle served as a bomber pilot with the Luftwaffe until his He 111 was shot

Jasta 60 leader Ltn Benzler was a recipient of the rarely-bestowed Lippe War Honour Cross for Heroic Deed, seen here pinned to his tunic next to his Iron Cross 1st Class. The OAW-built D VII in the background is believed to have been flown by Benzler, and it displays a white-edged dark fuselage band. Close inspection reveals the tail of another D VII in the hangar just to the right of Benzler's head, providing a view of the unit's chequerboard tailplane marking (HAC/UTD)

Jasta 60 personnel pose with a D VII (OAW) in October 1918. They are, from left to right, Vzfw Wunnenberg, Vzfw Zimmermann (one victory), Ltn Günther Dobberke (eight), Ltn d R Schwager, Ltn Benzler (CO, nine victories), Ltn d R Wolff (one), Ltn d R Ritscherle (eight), Vzfw Mack (one), Vzfw Bollemann and Vzfw Korff (eight). As in most such group photographs, the officers are in the centre, with the NCOs forming the 'book ends' on either side

Bullet hole patches in the popular form of small tricolour circles – some uncomfortably close to the cockpit – disfigure the fuselage insignia of Karl Ritscherle's OAW-built D VII of *Jasta* 60. Ritscherle used a black and white 'Mercedes star' to identify his machine, which also displays considerable fabric repair forward between the cockpit and metal cowling panels. The serial number is probably 4198/18 or possibly 4498/18. Ritscherle wears a Heinecke parachute harness

down over England on 24 August 1940. Having possibly baled out of his badly damaged bomber, Ritscherle subsequently drowned in the south Essex waterworks.

Jasta 81

Jadgstaffel 81 began its life as *Jagdflieger Ober-Ost* (Eastern Front) in June 1917. It was designated *Jasta* 81 that September and moved to the Western Front at the end of March 1918. Its leader from April to 24 August was Ltn Herbert Knappe, whose final two or three – of nine – victories were probably scored in a D VII before he was wounded. Fritz Höhn assumed temporary command, and he also claimed two kills before Oblt Pritsch took over on 3 September 1918.

Of the unit's war total of 40-odd victories, ten were scored by Vzfw Alfons Nagler, who was born in Ertingen, Württemburg, in August 1894. He had started his aviation career as a mechanic, but later became a two-seater pilot, moving to single-seaters with *Ober-Ost* before his transfer to France and *Jasta* 74. There, he gained one unconfirmed kill before rejoining his old unit, now re-named *Jasta* 81. Between May and October Nagler made nine more claims, the last five of which were possibly scored in a D VII.

Former two-seater pilot Vzfw Dietrich Averes was born in Nordhorn in January 1894. Also known as 'Derk', his first experience of fighters came with *Jagdflieger Ober-Ost*, with whom he *(text continues on page 64)*

COLOUR PLATES

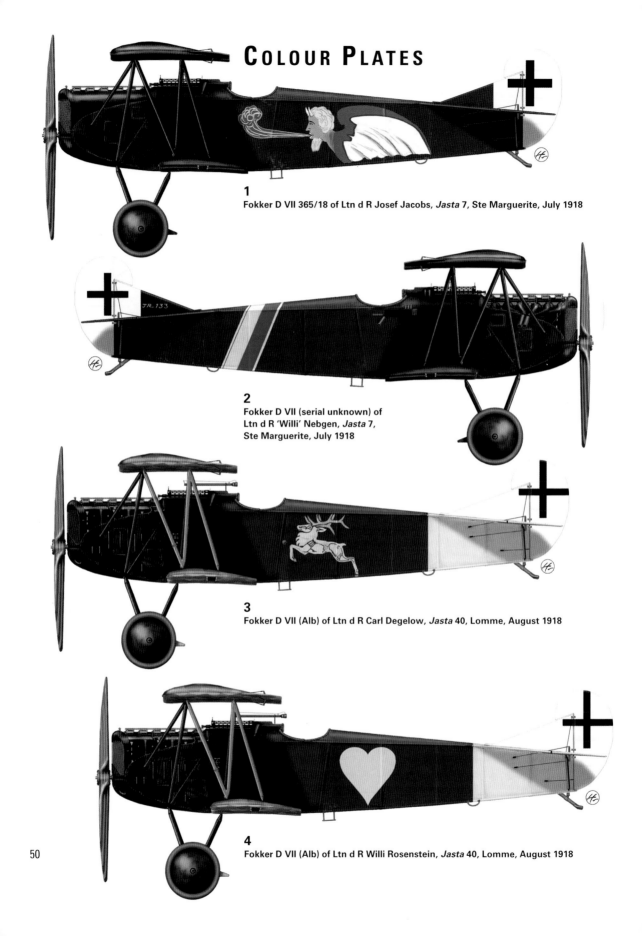

1
Fokker D VII 365/18 of Ltn d R Josef Jacobs, *Jasta* 7, Ste Marguerite, July 1918

2
Fokker D VII (serial unknown) of
Ltn d R 'Willi' Nebgen, *Jasta* 7,
Ste Marguerite, July 1918

3
Fokker D VII (Alb) of Ltn d R Carl Degelow, *Jasta* 40, Lomme, August 1918

4
Fokker D VII (Alb) of Ltn d R Willi Rosenstein, *Jasta* 40, Lomme, August 1918

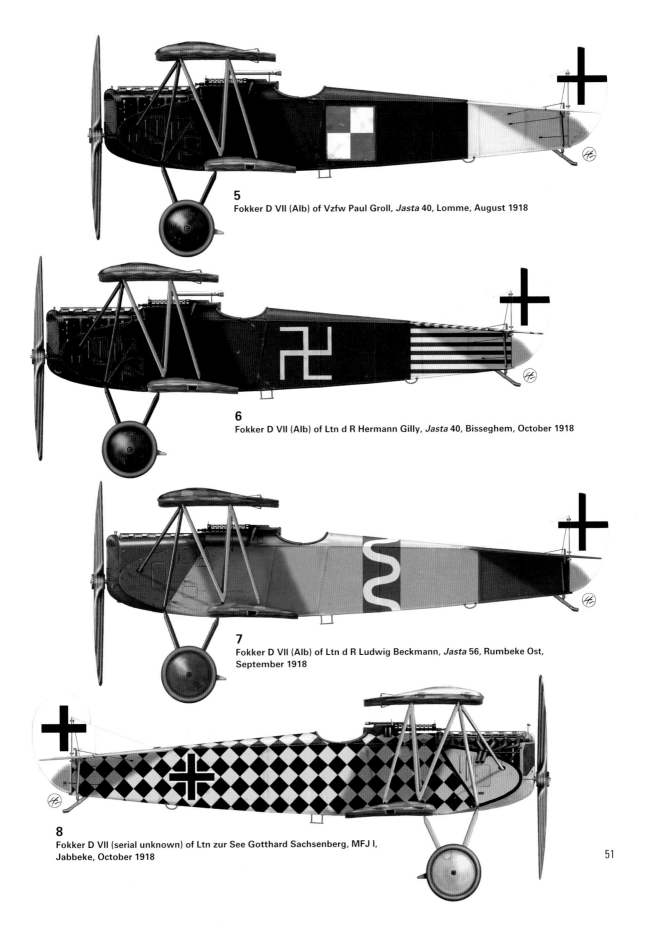

5
Fokker D VII (Alb) of Vzfw Paul Groll, *Jasta* 40, Lomme, August 1918

6
Fokker D VII (Alb) of Ltn d R Hermann Gilly, *Jasta* 40, Bisseghem, October 1918

7
Fokker D VII (Alb) of Ltn d R Ludwig Beckmann, *Jasta* 56, Rumbeke Ost,
September 1918

8
Fokker D VII (serial unknown) of Ltn zur See Gotthard Sachsenberg, MFJ I,
Jabbeke, October 1918

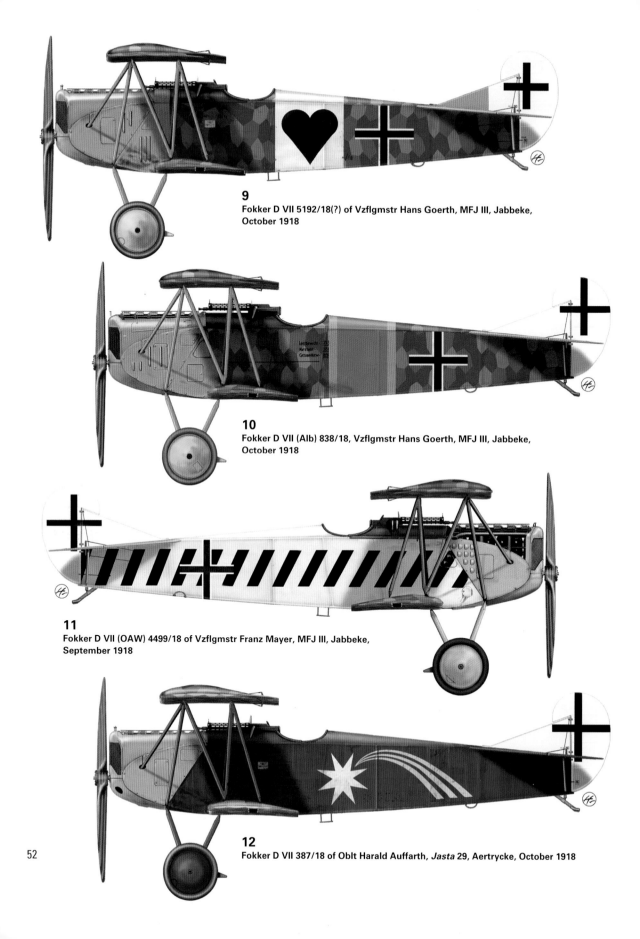

9
Fokker D VII 5192/18(?) of Vzflgmstr Hans Goerth, MFJ III, Jabbeke,
October 1918

10
Fokker D VII (Alb) 838/18, Vzflgmstr Hans Goerth, MFJ III, Jabbeke,
October 1918

11
Fokker D VII (OAW) 4499/18 of Vzflgmstr Franz Mayer, MFJ III, Jabbeke,
September 1918

12
Fokker D VII 387/18 of Oblt Harald Auffarth, *Jasta* 29, Aertrycke, October 1918

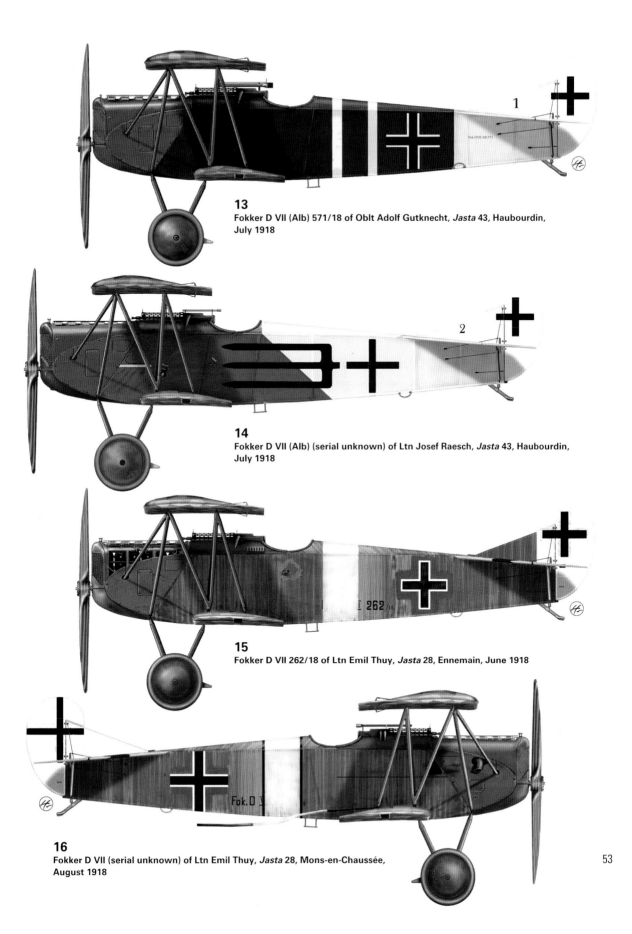

13
Fokker D VII (Alb) 571/18 of Oblt Adolf Gutknecht, *Jasta* 43, Haubourdin,
July 1918

14
Fokker D VII (Alb) (serial unknown) of Ltn Josef Raesch, *Jasta* 43, Haubourdin,
July 1918

15
Fokker D VII 262/18 of Ltn Emil Thuy, *Jasta* 28, Ennemain, June 1918

16
Fokker D VII (serial unknown) of Ltn Emil Thuy, *Jasta* 28, Mons-en-Chaussée,
August 1918

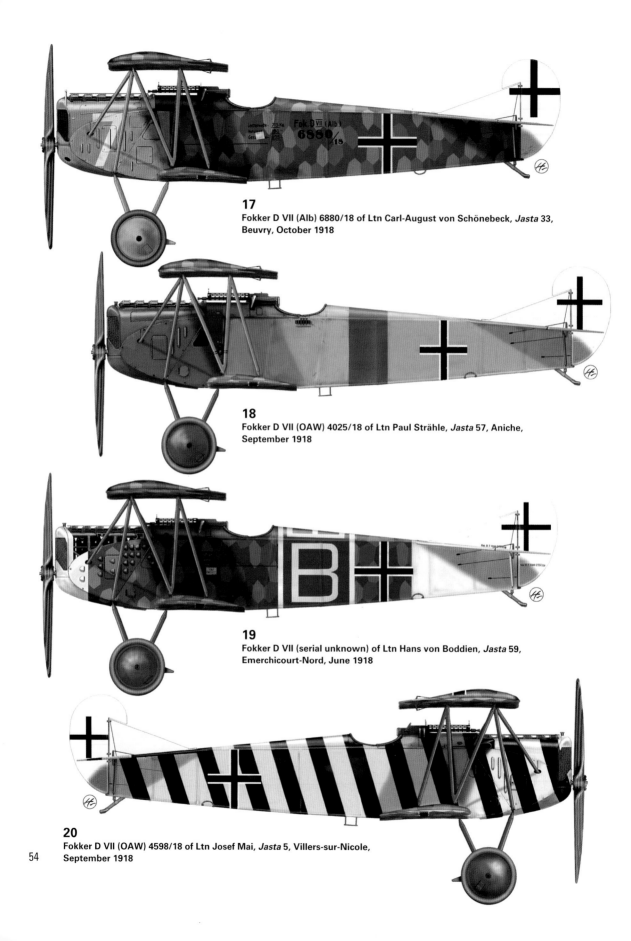

17
Fokker D VII (Alb) 6880/18 of Ltn Carl-August von Schönebeck, *Jasta* 33,
Beuvry, October 1918

18
Fokker D VII (OAW) 4025/18 of Ltn Paul Strähle, *Jasta* 57, Aniche,
September 1918

19
Fokker D VII (serial unknown) of Ltn Hans von Boddien, *Jasta* 59,
Emerchicourt-Nord, June 1918

20
Fokker D VII (OAW) 4598/18 of Ltn Josef Mai, *Jasta* 5, Villers-sur-Nicole,
September 1918

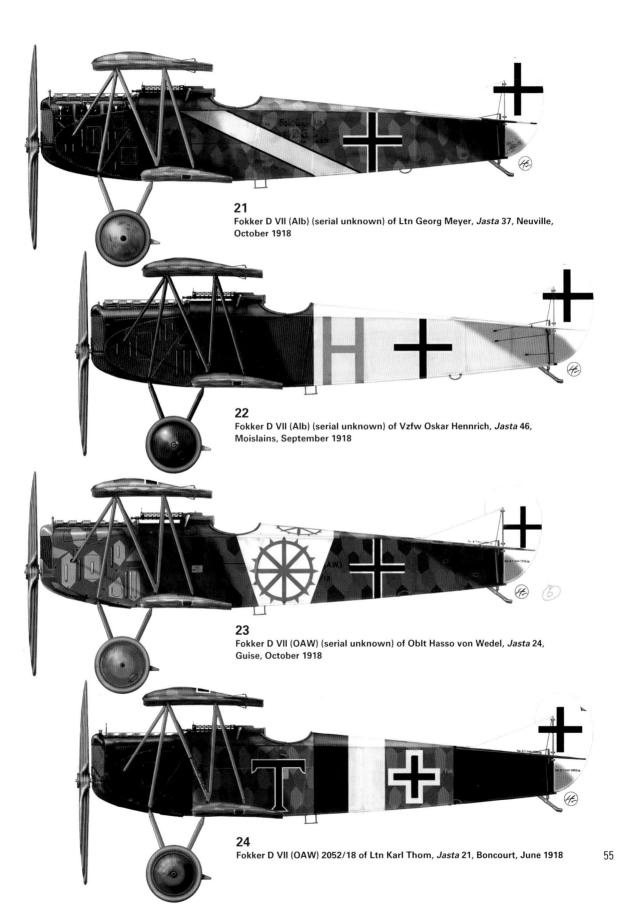

21
Fokker D VII (Alb) (serial unknown) of Ltn Georg Meyer, *Jasta* 37, Neuville,
October 1918

22
Fokker D VII (Alb) (serial unknown) of Vzfw Oskar Hennrich, *Jasta* 46,
Moislains, September 1918

23
Fokker D VII (OAW) (serial unknown) of Oblt Hasso von Wedel, *Jasta* 24,
Guise, October 1918

24
Fokker D VII (OAW) 2052/18 of Ltn Karl Thom, *Jasta* 21, Boncourt, June 1918

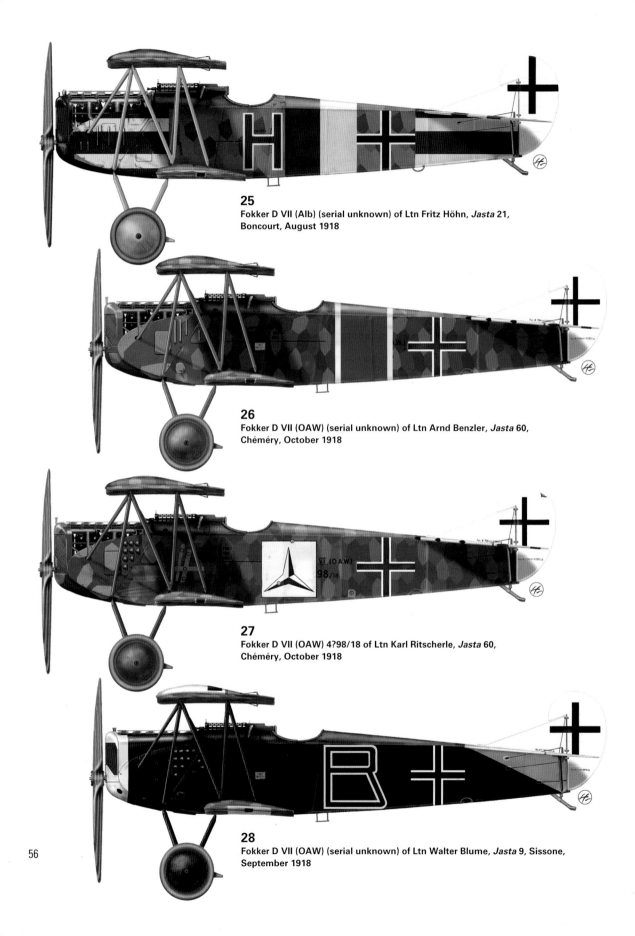

25
Fokker D VII (Alb) (serial unknown) of Ltn Fritz Höhn, *Jasta* 21,
Boncourt, August 1918

26
Fokker D VII (OAW) (serial unknown) of Ltn Arnd Benzler, *Jasta* 60,
Chémery, October 1918

27
Fokker D VII (OAW) 4?98/18 of Ltn Karl Ritscherle, *Jasta* 60,
Chémery, October 1918

28
Fokker D VII (OAW) (serial unknown) of Ltn Walter Blume, *Jasta* 9, Sissone,
September 1918

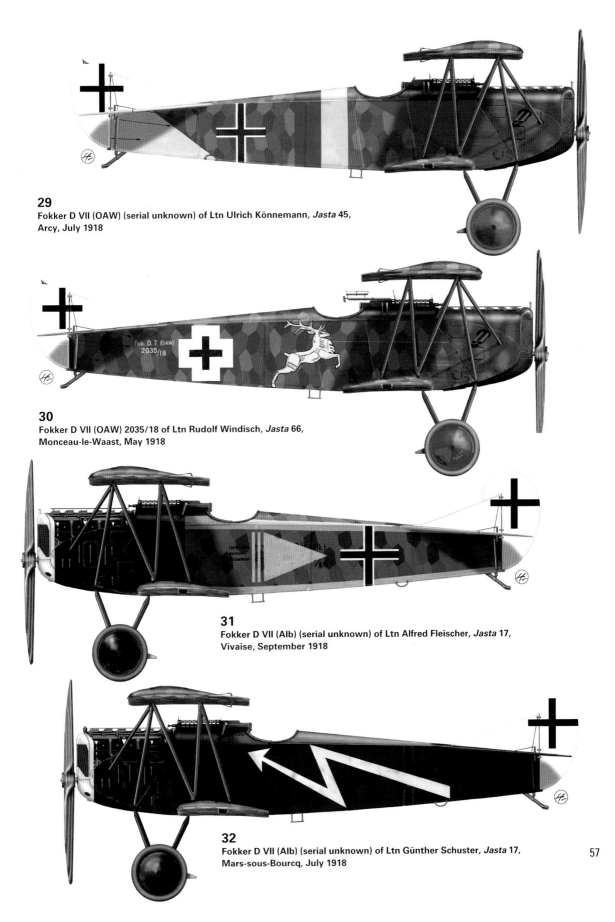

29
Fokker D VII (OAW) (serial unknown) of Ltn Ulrich Könnemann, *Jasta* 45,
Arcy, July 1918

30
Fokker D VII (OAW) 2035/18 of Ltn Rudolf Windisch, *Jasta* 66,
Monceau-le-Waast, May 1918

31
Fokker D VII (Alb) (serial unknown) of Ltn Alfred Fleischer, *Jasta* 17,
Vivaise, September 1918

32
Fokker D VII (Alb) (serial unknown) of Ltn Günther Schuster, *Jasta* 17,
Mars-sous-Bourcq, July 1918

57

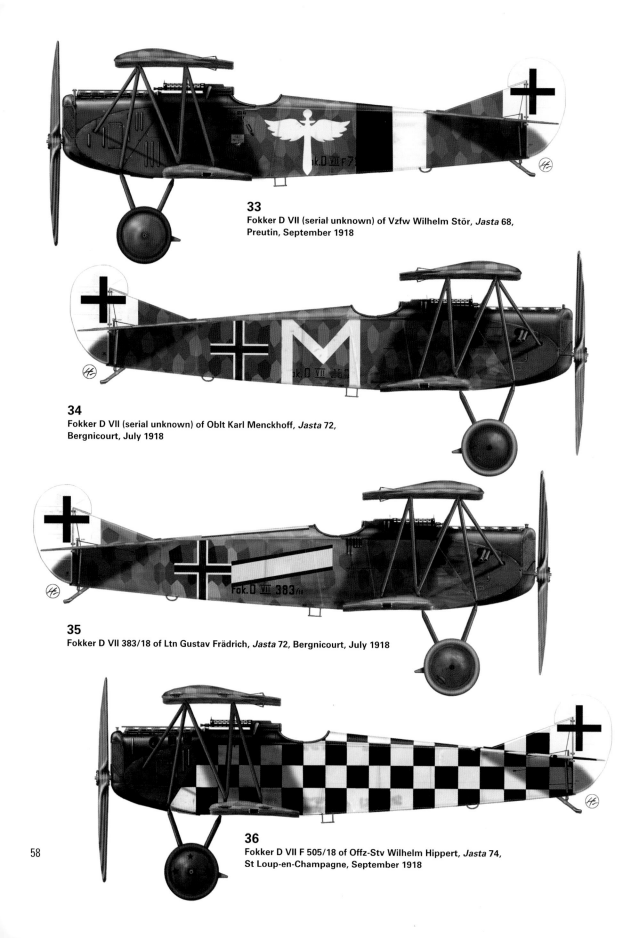

33
Fokker D VII (serial unknown) of Vzfw Wilhelm Stör, *Jasta* 68,
Preutin, September 1918

34
Fokker D VII (serial unknown) of Oblt Karl Menckhoff, *Jasta* 72,
Bergnicourt, July 1918

35
Fokker D VII 383/18 of Ltn Gustav Frädrich, *Jasta* 72, Bergnicourt, July 1918

36
Fokker D VII F 505/18 of Offz-Stv Wilhelm Hippert, *Jasta* 74,
St Loup-en-Champagne, September 1918

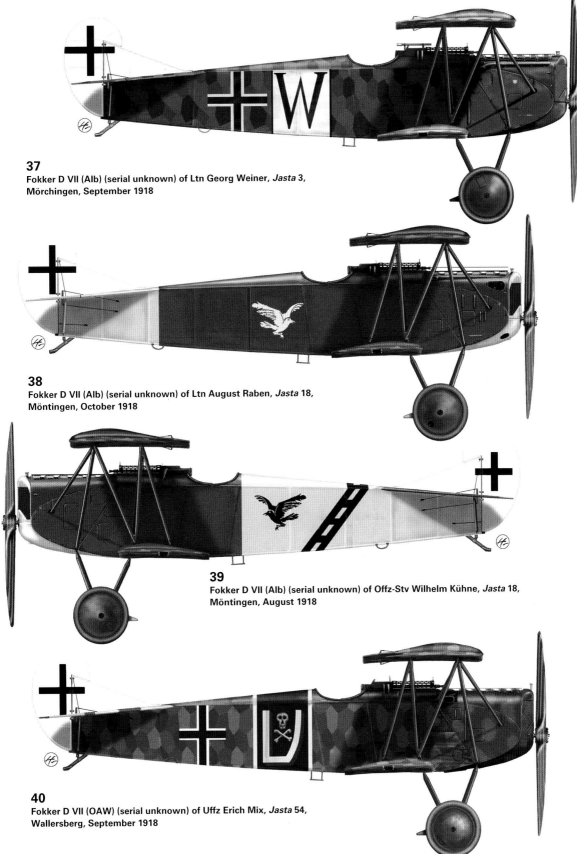

37
Fokker D VII (Alb) (serial unknown) of Ltn Georg Weiner, *Jasta* 3,
Mörchingen, September 1918

38
Fokker D VII (Alb) (serial unknown) of Ltn August Raben, *Jasta* 18,
Möntingen, October 1918

39
Fokker D VII (Alb) (serial unknown) of Offz-Stv Wilhelm Kühne, *Jasta* 18,
Möntingen, August 1918

40
Fokker D VII (OAW) (serial unknown) of Uffz Erich Mix, *Jasta* 54,
Wallersberg, September 1918

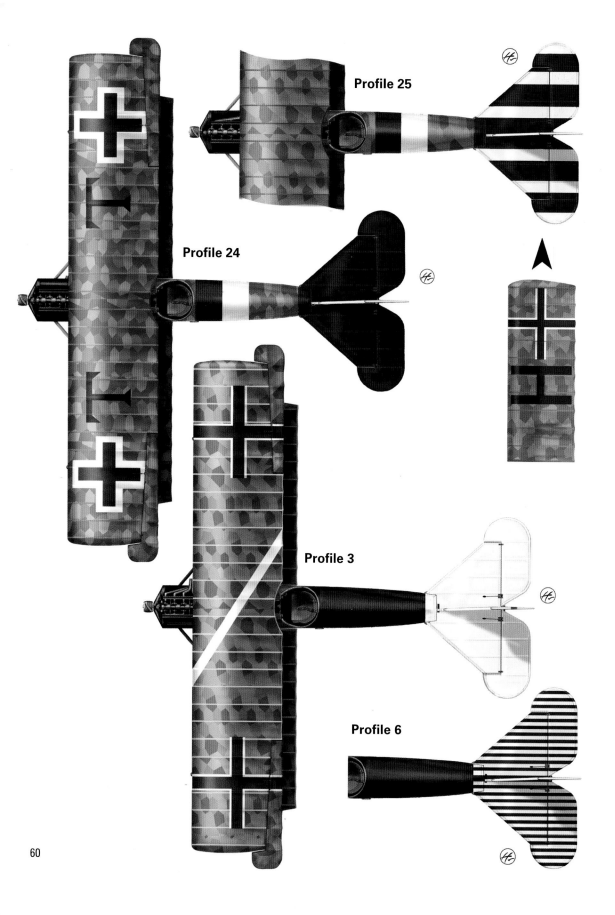

Profile 25

Profile 24

Profile 3

Profile 6

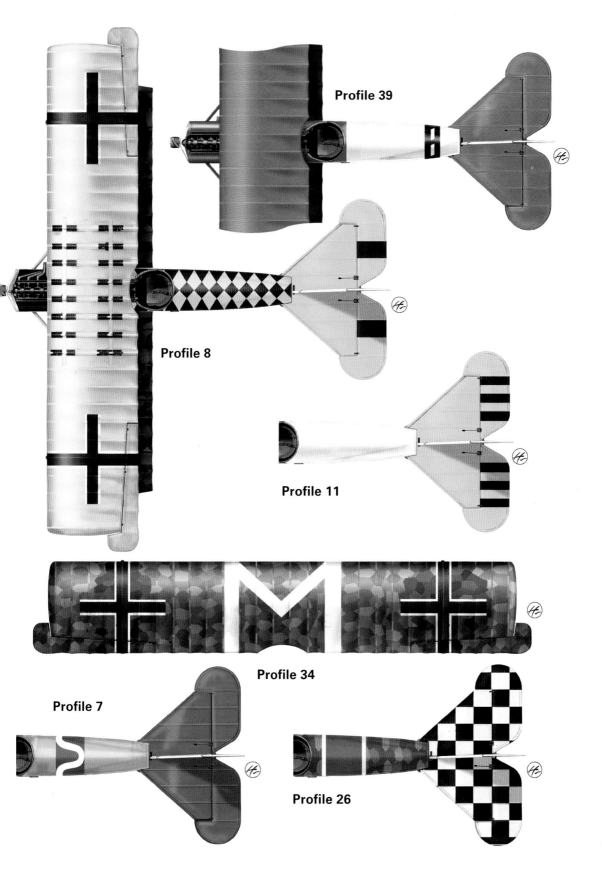

Profile 39

Profile 8

Profile 11

Profile 34

Profile 7

Profile 26

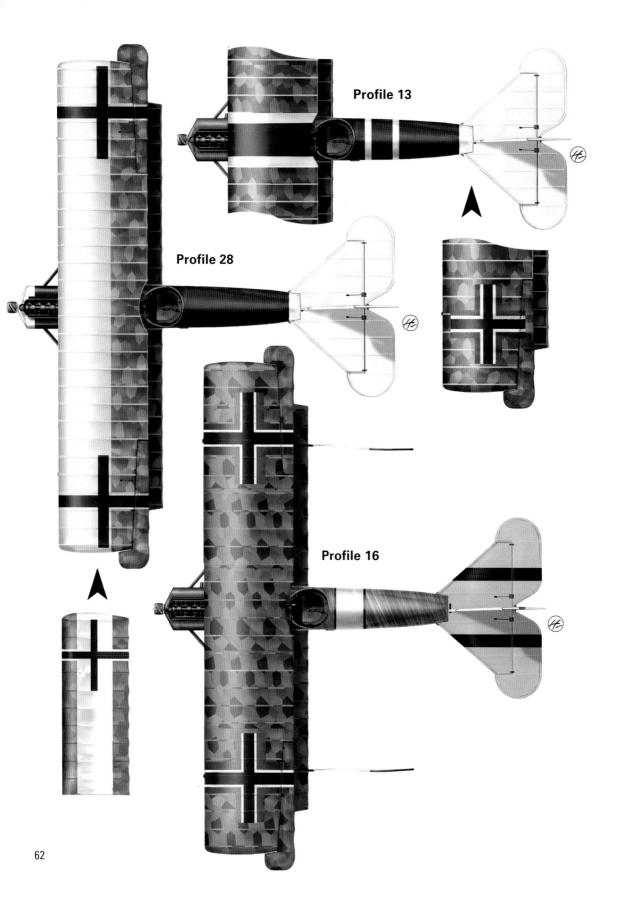

Profile 13

Profile 28

Profile 16

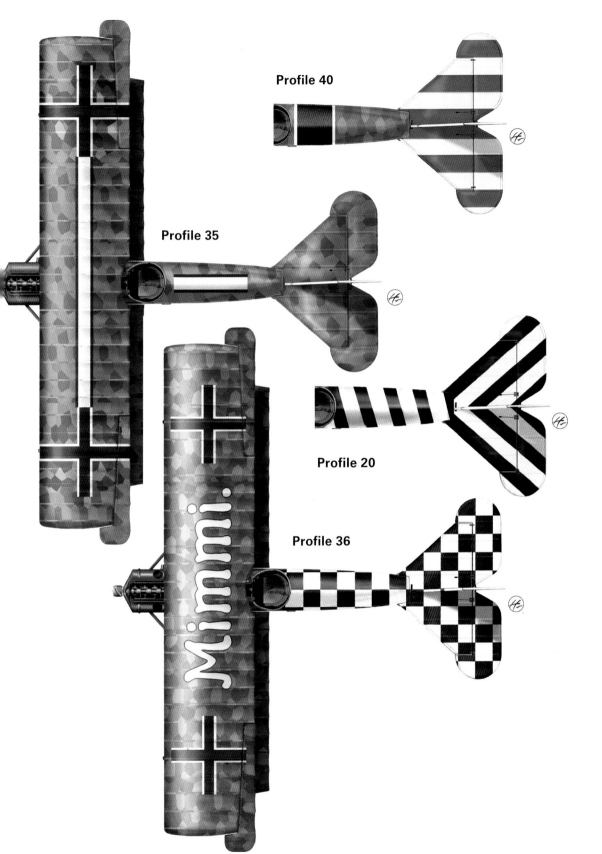

Profile 40

Profile 35

Profile 20

Profile 36

claimed a balloon destroyed on the Eastern Front, prior to the unit becoming *Jasta* 81 and moving to France. There, Averes raised his score to ten, of which the last seven were probably achieved while flying the D VII. There is, however, a suggestion that his score may have been as high as 19. Averes was an active glider pilot between the wars, and served in the Luftwaffe as a major in World War 2. He eventually passed away in September 1982.

7th ARMY – JAGDGRUPPE Nr 5

From 12 August to 23 September 1918, *Jagdgruppe Nr 5*, commanded by *Rittmeister* Konstantin von Braun, included *Jagdstaffeln* 9, 41, 45, 50 and 66. From 29 September to war's end, *Jastas* 9, 21s, 45 and 66 became 7th Army's *Jagdgruppe Armee Ost*, with Ltn H J Rolfes being its CO.

Jasta 9

Ltn d R Walter Blume had led *Jasta* 9 since 1918, and he was its star performer. From Hirschberg, Silesia, he saw action with the 5th Silesian *Jäger* Battalion soon after war was declared and, following an early wound, transferred to the air service in June 1915. In 1961 he provided a detailed account of his wartime aviation career;

'Having completed my training as a flier in early June 1916, I was transferred to the front to join F. Fl. Abt. 65, flying Aviatik two-seaters. I served with this group from 18 June 1916 through to 20 January 1917, and was awarded the Iron Cross, 2nd Class on 24 July 1916. I requested, and obtained, a transfer to the newly-formed *Jagdstaffel* 26 on 20 January

A great deal of talent – with drinks all around – are on hand during this gathering of airmen from *Jagdgruppen* 4 and 5 of the 7th Army, circa August 1918. They are, to the left of the steps, Ltn Werner Preuss of *Jasta* 66 (22 victories) and Ltn Benzler of *Jasta* 60 (eight), and in front of the steps, Ltn d R Blume of *Jasta* 9 (28) and Oblt von Kalkreuth (the *Jasta* 21 OzbV). Seated is Ltn Schlenker of *Jasta* 41 (14), on the first step, between Blume and Kalkreuth, unknown, on the second, his hand on Blume's shoulder, is von Boenigk (26) and Ltn Christians of *Jasta* 21 (two), and on the third are Ltn d R Hans Joachim Rolfes of *Jasta* 45 (16) and Fritz Höhn of *Jastas* 21, 60 and 41 (21 victories). The four at the top are unknown, Ltn Schlumps, Ltn Julius Keller of *Jasta* 21 (two victories) and Ltn Rupke, an adjutant from *Grufl* 5

Jasta 9 personnel gather in front of one of their D VIIs, which has been festooned with greenery to commemorate the unit's 100th victory. They are, from left to right, unknown, Vzfw Karl Strünklenberg, Ltn Herbert Rolle, *Staffelführer* Walter Blume, unknown, Ltn Dorn, and Ltn Galander
(A Imrie via HAC/UTD)

On 30 September 1918 Ltn d R Walter Blume was awarded the *Pour le Mérite,* and the *Jasta* 9 leader proudly displays the order in this fine view. Blume began his career as a *jagdflieger* in *Jasta* 26, and after gaining six victories there, he was sidelined by a chest wound for several months. He returned to command *Jasta* 9 and survived the war with 28 victories to his name *(HAC/UTD)*

The original caption to this photograph stated that the smiling Walter Blume was removing his tunic after scoring *Jasta* 9's 100th and his 25th victory on 14 September 1918. At the extreme left is Ltn Galander. Blume's OAW-built Fokker, which displays his stylised 'B' marking on the black fuselage, has a white radiator shell and tail. Just visible on the original print of this photograph is the leading half of the upper wing surface in white, between the horizontal cross arms. A similar decoration may have been applied to the underside of the lower wings, but this cannot be confirmed *(A Imrie)*

1917, where I served under Oblt Bruno Loerzer. On 30 January 1917 I was promoted to leutnant. The aircraft we flew during this period were all Albatros – D IIs, D IIIs and D Vs. I gained six confirmed victories with this *Staffel* and was decorated with the Iron Cross 1st Class on 14 August 1917. I was severely wounded in combat over the Houthulst Forest on 29 November 1917 and spent approximately three-and-a-half months recovering from my wounds.

'On 5 March 1918 I was made CO of *Jagdstaffel* 9, succeeding Oblt Kurt Student, and I continued with the squadron until the end of the war, gaining a total of 28 confirmed enemy aircraft destroyed. I was decorated with the "Hohenzollern", with Crown and Swords, as well as the *Pour le Mérite* (on 30 September). Our Fokker D VII aircraft had black fuselages, white radiators and white wings. In addition to these colours, my aircraft bore a large letter "B" on the side of the fuselage.'

After the war Blume went into engineering and worked as an aircraft designer with the Albatros and Arado companies, as well as taking up gliding. He died in May 1964

Jasta 41

Fritz Höhn from *Jasta* 60 assumed leadership of *Jasta* 41 on 1 October 1918 but was killed two days later. He had apparently added three victories to his score, one on each of his last three days. Ltn Helmut Brünig from *Jasta* 50 then became CO.

Former infantryman, Vzfw Josef Schwendemann had been with *Jasta* 41 since September 1917, moving from *Schutzstaffel* 14. Scoring steadily since the beginning of 1918, he had claimed 12 victories by the time the D VIIs arrived. Details of his final five claims are not known, but most, if not all, would have been achieved with the new Fokker fighter.

Jasta 45

One of the most effective *Staffeln* in 1918, *Jasta* 45 achieved at least 113 victories that year, including 28 balloons. The first Fokkers arrived in June and were gratefully received by the *Staffelführer*, Ltn Hans Joachim

Rolfes, who had commanded the unit from its formation. Unusually, Rolfes had been born in Port Elizabeth, South Africa, the son of the German Consul, and was educated both there and in London. He went to Germany in 1912 to enlist in the dragoons and was commissioned soon after the outbreak of war. Severely wounded in August 1915, he moved to the aviation service and flew two-seaters in Russia and France. Rolfes arrived at *Jasta* 32 with one unconfirmed kill, and he duly gained his first confirmed victory with this unit. Appointed to command *Jasta* 45, he stayed with the unit until the end of the war. By the time the first D VIIs arrived, Rolfes' victory score had risen to eight, and he more than doubled this to 17 by the Armistice. In the last weeks of the war he commanded *Jagdgruppe Armee Ost* but did not add to his score. Rolfes was killed in a flying accident at Johannisthal, Berlin, on 12 August 1935.

Jasta 45's most accomplished pilot, however, was Ltn Gustav Dörr, who failed to receive a well deserved *Pour le Mérite* due to the award's recommendation having not been approved before war's end. Born in October 1887, he was 31 years old by the Armistice, having achieved an impressive 35 victories and others unconfirmed. Dörr had joined the army in 1908, and on the outbreak of war he immediately saw combat with *Infanterie Regiment Nr 76*. Wounded in the first week of the conflict, he would be hospitalised twice more due to enemy action while serving in the infantry.

Dörr transferred to the aviation service in July 1915, and he flew two-seaters until he suffered serious facial injuries in a bad crash in June 1917. In February 1918 he went to *Jasta* 45 and, after his third victory, he was lucky to survive being shot down in flames. By August Dörr was scoring heavily against SPADs, Bréguets and Salmsons, and five days after his 23rd kill, on the 24th of that month, he received the Golden Military Merit Cross. Commissioned in September, his successes continued into the autumn, with victory number 35 falling to Dörr's guns on 30 October. He survived the war, but died in an accident in December 1928.

Jasta **45 operated a mixed bag of aircraft in June 1918, this line-up consisting of six new OAW-built D VIIs and five Albatros fighters at the far end. The Fokkers display the obliquely-marked unit colours on their noses and tails.** Jasta **45 was commanded by Hans Joachim Rolfes throughout its war service, the ace contributing 16 of the unit's 113 victories**

One of the older fighter pilots of his day, 35-kill ace Gustav Dörr was 31 by war's end. Fighting as an NCO for much of the conflict, the Jasta **45 pilot just missed out on a well-deserved 'Blue Max'**

Vzfw Karl Paul Schlegel was another star NCO pilot of *Jasta* 45, scoring at least 22 victories, of which 14 were balloons. He died after attacking a French balloon on 27 October 1918, possibly falling to Sous Lt Pierre Marinovitch of SPA 94 *(Franks collection)*

Ltn Ulrich Könnemann contributed four victories to the *Jasta* 45 total, probably all with the D VII. His OAW-built Fokker shows the diagonal demarcation of the unit's nose colour, as well as his own personal marking of a vertical two-tone band. The fuselage cross was of 4:5 proportions *(USAFM)*

Another successful *Jasta* 45 NCO pilot was Saxon Vzfw Karl Paul Schlegel, who was born in Wechselburg in May 1893. An army cadet from 1907, he also saw action within days of the war commencing, fighting in both France and Russia. As a member of *Maschinengewehr-Abteilung* 8, he had received Saxony's Silver St Henry medal in April 1915. In the spring of 1917 Schlegel transferred to the air service, and by May he was with *Jasta* 45. His first three victories were claimed over balloons and by the end of July his score has risen to 12, half of them balloons. Flying the D VII, Schlegel went on to destroy another eight balloons and two aircraft.

Enjoying a friendly rivalry with Dörr, he took his score to 22, with at least three more not confirmed (two on the day he was killed). He, too, won the Golden Military Merit Cross. On 27 October Schlegel was, as usual, flying with Dörr, and he had apparently downed a balloon and a SPAD. After Dörr was forced to leave with mechanical trouble, Schlegel's aircraft was seen to dive into the ground. He may have been the 19th victim of French ace Sous Lt Pierre Marinovitch of SPA 94.

Gefr Johan Schlimpen from Daun, near Cologne, became an ace with *Jasta* 45, and it is possible that most of his five victories were achieved in a D VII. Schlimpen was killed near Fismes on 20 August.

Ltn Ulrich Könnemann was certainly victor over four aircraft during the time *Jasta* 45 operated the D VII, and he may well have become an ace with a fifth kill, scored on 14 October 1918, but records are incomplete for the final weeks of the war. A former Hussar, the 20-year-old Könnemann came from Wittenburg, and he had gone through the usual route of flying two-seaters in 1917.

Jasta 50

Ltn Hans von Freden, commander of *Jasta* 50, was born in Berlin in March 1892. Having begun his war with the artillery, he had served with flak units from 1916 until he switched to aviation. Trained as an observer, von Freden was soon wounded after joining his first unit. He was eventually assigned to fighters with *Jasta* 1 in Italy in November 1917, where he scored three victories before returning to France to fly with *Jasta*

72. When *Jasta* 1 was posted back to the Western Front, von Freden returned to his old unit and added a fourth claim to his tally.

Appointed to command *Jasta* 50 in June 1918, he had a score of around ten by the time the D VIIs arrived. Between then and war's end von Freden doubled his total to twenty, nine of which were balloons. He may well have received the 'Blue Max' had the war not ended, but in any event he did not live long to savour his successes for he died on 30 October 1919 during the great influenza pandemic.

After the war one of von Freden's pilots, Uffz Vahldieck (under the pseudonym 'Wilfried Eck'), wrote some recollections of his time with *Jasta* 50 under the title *Luftkämpfe im Westen*, which O'Brien Browne has translated. One incident, although noted as 29 September 1918, probably occurred three days earlier. He wrote;

Officers of *Jasta* 50 form the back row in this group photograph, while the NCOs are seated in front, along with the inevitable mascot. They are, back row, from left to right, Ltn Harbst (the OzbV), Ltn d R von Melle, *Staffelführer* Ltn d R Hans von Freden (16 victories), Ltn von Buddeberg (one), Ltn d R Karl Maletsky (four) and Ltn Dörr (not to be confused with the *Jasta* 45 ace). Front row, from left to right, Uffz Vahldieck, Flieger Schnitzer, Gefr Röhr (one) and Flieger Reganzk. The OAW-built D VII may be von Freden's, which bears his family coat of arms *(HAC/UTD)*

Hans von Freden, *Jagdstaffel* 50 CO, stands fifth from right in this group. The D VII (OAW) behind them displays the unit's marking of a (possibly) black chevron on the white tailplane and a matching stripe on the white fuselage beneath the tail

68

Vzfw Karl Weinmann of *Jasta* 50 set out to attack a French balloon on the morning of 26 September 1918 but the tables were turned. Before he could set the balloon on fire, he was shot down near Ville-sur-Tourbe by Capt Armand de Turenne of SPA 12. Weinmann landed his D VII (OAW) intact, thus permitting the French ace (at left) to pose with the prize, which represented his 15th, and final, victory. The *Jasta* 50 unit marking of a (possibly) black chevron on a white tail is well displayed, as is the personal zig-zag two-tone stripe marking on the fuselage. A white 'F' is painted on the wing centre section. Note that the fuselage cross has already been removed for a souvenir and the same has probably been done with the Albatros logo on the rudder. The upper wing cross was altered from a previous thicker version *(SHAA)*

'It was bustling in the early morning of 29 September 1918 at the Boncourt airfield. The trucks of *Jagdstaffel* 50 were packed high – airfields were to be changed once again. The tents had already been taken down and the assembled men hurried busily here and there to make the objects entrusted to them ready for a fight against the enemy. The aircraft were in a long row, lined up as if on parade, and they waited for the gentlemen pilots who were not yet to be seen. A peaceful observer would, with a look at these storm birds, be overcome by a strange feeling. They looked wild in their colourful war paint.

'One had a death's head as decoration, another a family coat of arms (Ltn von Freden), a pig with a cloverleaf in its snout (Ltn Dörr), a skull (Ltn Schädel), a comet with a tail (Ltn Maletsky), a shovel and spade (Uffz Nimszyk) and so on, each according to the imagination of the pilot concerned. And then they themselves came rushing up, dashing, weather-bronzed figures. The cars hadn't even fully halted and they were already out of them.

'"*Die herren Piloten, bitte*", called Ltn von Freden. "*Meine Herren*, a French offensive will begin today in the 3rd Army sector in Champagne. We will be transferred there and move to the airfield at Leffincourt this morning. I ask you to make yourselves ready – we take off in five minutes. Thank you very much".

'Soon the pilots are sitting in their aircraft, letting their motors run one more time and listening to their powerful song. Everything is in order. Then the corporal in charge of the take off steps up to the lead fighter.

'"*Staffel* ready for flight!"

'"Fire the flare for take off!"

'With a wild run, the fighters move forward to form up in the air. Just an honorary pass over the village of Boncourt, where they have spent such fine hours, then it was to the front, over the old airfield at Sissonne and the giant field hospital facilities lying next to it. Soon the *Staffel* saw the old royal city of Reims with its proud cathedral, and the way led further on over Soissons – everything is shot-up, destroyed.

'Below lay Champagne, criss-crossed by the white lines of the trenches. The entire area is covered as if by a fog. French artillery is firing wherever the eye sees. Then, a firm will grows inside the pilots – to support their comrades on the ground. Ltn von Freden turns his gaze to the south-east to get his orientation. He wants to look over the terrible battlefield once again, where he was startled – one, two, three, at least 40 enemy fighters . . . the Germans are only 13!

'Von Freden pulled his fighter into a bank and his *Kette*, consisting of six aircraft, set themselves behind him in defensive formation, forming into a circle. The French fly towards the German swarm several times but receive a respectable machine gun fire right on the nose. Then the French squadron leader thrusts into the middle of the squadron and flies through it. Gefr Röhr lets himself be tempted into following the Frenchman but the latter is quicker, and soon Röhr is flying away with a thick cloud of smoke, but he can land all right.

'In the meantime, the *Staffel* is caught up in a hard fight. As the swirling mass was at its greatest, the second swarm, led by Ltn Buddeberg, pushes in from above. Surprised, the Frenchmen break off their attack. Three burning aircraft are heading down to the ground. Friend or foe?

'The fighters circle wildly around each other, searching for an opponent's weakness. Nothing happens in such a banking fight of several machines because everyone must be careful that he doesn't get rammed. Flare after flare blazed forth from von Freden's aircraft. That slowly unsnarled the tangle, and everyone pushes over to his side. Astounded, von Freden, counts his trusty followers and, except for Röhr, he can make out no casualties. And now quickly home. A few minutes later one Fokker after the other rolls across the Leffincourt airfield. One aircraft lost, three aerial victories won – von Freden two, Ltn Maletsky one.'

Jasta 50 moved to Leffincourt on 25 September and Maletsky scored two victories over SPADs on the 26th.

After a brief stay with *Jasta* 32, Ltn Helmut Brünig moved to *Jasta* 50 in January 1918. Already an ace by 22 July, he probably added his last two kills flying the D VII to bring his score to seven.

Jasta 66

Jasta 66 acquired at least one new D VII in late May 1918, and its leader, Rudolf Windisch (already victor of 22 combats), was keen to take it into battle. On 27 May he led his men in D VII (OAW) 2035/18, which was adorned with a white stag emblem similar to that displayed by Degelow of *Jasta* 40. This marking was based on the emblem of a sanatorium and health resort in Dresden called *Bad Weisser Hirsch*. Windisch and Degelow had spent time there recovering from wounds.

Born in Dresden on 27 January 1897, 'Rudi' Windisch had transferred to the aviation service from the infantry after being wounded by grenade fragments on 21 November 1914. He first flew with F. Fl. Abt. 62, where he met fellow Saxon Max Immelmann. After this unit transferred to the Eastern Front, Windisch gained notoriety for a daring mission flown on 2 October 1916.

Landing his Roland C II behind Russian lines at dawn, Windisch dropped off his observer, Oblt Maximilian von Cossel, who then hiked to

Rudolf Windisch of *Jasta* 66 smiles from the cockpit of his brand new D VII (OAW) 2035/18 in May 1918, shortly before his mysterious demise. This example of a very early OAW-built Fokker displays the white stag emblem, based (like Degelow's insignia) on the crest of *Dr Lahmann's Sanatorium in Weisser Hirsch* in Windisch's native Dresden. Four-colour fabric covers the aircraft, which has a cheek rest to aid use of the tubular sight

As a two-seater pilot, 'Rudi' Windisch was highly decorated for a daring mission deep into Russian territory in 1916. By the time he flew the D VII as *Jasta* 66 CO, he had accumulated 21 victories and been recommended for the *Pour le Mérite*. On 27 May 1918 he was brought down behind French lines in his D VII (OAW) 2052/18. He was never heard from again, and the circumstances surrounding his fate remain unclear to this day

In spite of this crudely-retouched photograph, Ltn Werner Preuss of *Jasta* 66 failed to receive the *Pour le Mérite* because his nomination came too late. He survived the war with 22 victories, but died in a flying accident on 6 March 1919 *(Franks collection)*

the Russian railway line between Dubnow and Rowno. There, he set explosive charges under the track which he detonated as a train passed by, severely disrupting troop transport in the area. Von Cossel was then picked up by Windisch at a pre-arranged area the next morning. Windisch was awarded the Prussian Crown Order IV Class with Swords for the deed and was transferred to *Kagohl* II, on the Western Front.

In February 1917 he became a fighter pilot with *Jasta* 32, and after scoring eight victories was appointed commander of *Jasta* 66 after a brief stint with *Jasta* 50. By 27 May 1918 Windisch's combat score had reached 21, and the recommendation for his 'Blue Max' had been forwarded. However, he failed to return from his first patrol in the new D VII on this day and the medal was never awarded.

Fellow pilot Werner Preuss later wrote to Windisch's father about the events of 27 May, when *Jasta* 66 encountered French SPADs;

'We were barely out of the haze when we immediately saw nine SPAD single-seaters and several two-seaters in front of us. Your son immediately took on a two-seater. He managed to pressure the opponent down and several single-seaters got behind him and fired, but they were at such a distance that we could not hit them because we were shooting without telescopic sights. But the Frenchmen, who were fitted with excellent telescopic sights, were already starting to fire, often at great distances. And, in fact, sometimes they also had some luck. Such an accidental hit must have hit the fuel tank of your son's 'plane. Then suddenly we saw him go down in spirals and land. I could see how he was obviously making an intentional crash-landing to prevent the enemy from capturing an intact aeroplane.'

Jasta 66 pilot Vzfw Erich Sonneck applied for a victory on his leader's behalf, but kills were rarely credited to pilots who failed to return. Preuss also wrote ;

'I saw four hostile aircraft lying completely destroyed on the meadow between Lesges and Courvrelles. In the same meadow lay a Fokker D VII. Of the four enemy aircraft, two were shot down by Ltn Turck, one by Vzfw Peters and one by Ltn Windisch.'

Because it was thought that Windisch had survived his forced landing, his recommendation for the 'Blue Max' was not cancelled and its approval came through on 6 June. However, Windisch never returned, and the French never confirmed his death either. This would seem to support the theory that while he got down safely, he was either shot out of hand, or was killed trying to escape, either then or while a captive.

Werner Preuss, born in September 1894, had yet to score on the day he saw Windisch fall, but did gain his first victory nine days later. Whether he immediately flew a D VII is not certain, but he certainly acquired one fairly quickly and was an ace by July. Preuss was yet another infantryman turned aviator, transferring to the air service in September 1917. Like his erstwhile CO, Preuss' final tally was 22 kills. He too was recommended for the *Pour lé Merite,* but failed to receive it before the war ended. Nor did he survive long, being killed in a flying accident on 6 March 1919.

Arthur Laumann was another successful *Jasta* 66 pilot. He began his fighter career with the *Jasta* in May 1918, became an ace in July and, by month's end, had 15 victories. When Laumann left the unit on 14 August (with a score of 24), he had been in command since 21 July.

He went on to command *Jasta* 10 within JG I, bringing his score to 28. Laumann received the *Pour le Mérite* in October.

Paul Turck had started scoring with *Jasta* 66, having joined it in January 1918. He held temporary command for most of August, and ended the war, back with *Jasta* 21, with ten kills. Erich Sonneck also joined *Jasta* 66 in January 1918 and scored six victories, five of them possibly while flying D VIIs. Meanwhile, Vzfw Otto Bieleit, who came to the unit from *Jasta* 45 with one victory, scored four more with *Jasta* 66 – three

SPADs and two Bréguets. *Jasta* 66 was one of the most successful *Staffeln* in the war's last year, its pilots claiming 98 victories.

1st ARMY – *JAGDGRUPPE* LENZ

Operational between 11 July and 8 August 1918, *Jagdgruppe* Lenz was formed from *Jastas* 22s, 63, 69 and 76b. Its CO, Ltn Alfred Lenz, was an old warhorse, having flown two-seaters since the war's early days and then served under Rudolf Berthold with *Kampfeinsitzer-Kommando-Süd*, which later became *Jasta* 4. Although Lenz took command of *Jasta* 22 in July 1917, he did not score another victory until April 1918. Indeed, when *Jasta* 22 became part of JGr Lenz for four weeks or so, it only scored four victories before moving as JGr 5 to the 2nd Army Front. Lenz ended the war with six kills, most of which had been scored in mid-1918.

Two of JGr Lenz's victories were scored by Vzfw Karl Bohnenkamp for his fifth and sixth kills. Becoming a *jagdflieger* via the two-seater route, this NCO pilot joined *Jasta* 22 in July 1917, and by the end of the war had 15 victories (ten would probably have been scored flying a D VII).

1st AND 5th ARMIES – *JAGDGRUPPE Nr* 1

Led by Hptm Constantin von Bentheim, *Jagdgruppe Nr* 1 had been operating with the 4th and 18th armies since the summer of 1917, controlling various *Jastas*. During the Fokker D VII era, it operated with 1st Army and later the 5th. From 11 July 1918 *Jagdgruppe Nr* 1 comprised *Jastas* 8, 31, 62, 68, 72s, 73 and 74. After 15 September it transferred to 5th Army, opposite Verdun, with *Jastas* 8, 62, 68, and 74.

Jasta 8

Ltn Werner Junck was made *Jasta* 8 *Staffelführer* in April 1918, by which time he had served with the unit for a year – he was only credited with one confirmed kill in that time. However, by September he had increased his score to five (probably with three victories on the D VII), all of which were SPADs. Junck was a Luftwaffe generalleutnant in World War 2 and he died in August 1976.

Another pilot who gained a few final victories with the D VII, taking his score to 15, was Ltn Rudolf Francke. But the only *Jasta* 8 pilot to gain at least five victories with the Fokker was NCO pilot Wilhelm Anton Seitz. He had served with the unit almost since its formation, and scored steadily so that his tally reached five on 24 March 1918. Seitz had doubled his score by 23 August 1918, and between September and November he added six more kills and was also commissioned.

Jasta 31

Only one D VII ace emerged from *Jasta* 31, and that was after the unit had left *Jagdgruppe Nr* 1. Nonetheless, he is noteworthy for the fact that he was Polish. Ltn Mieczyslaw Sylwester Garsztka was born on 31 December 1896 in Bydgoszcz, and he had served with the German 84th Infantry Regiment since 1915. Joining the air service in 1917, Garsztka was assigned to *Jasta* 31 in July 1918 and had scored his first kill by the time the D VIIs arrived. On 1 September, the *Jasta* was detached from JGr 1 and transferred to Guise. Garsztka added a further five victories in September, but was wounded on 2 October and did not return to the front.

Post-war, he helped establish the Polish Air Force, serving as an instructor at Poznan-Lawica. Garsztka returned to combat in the war between Poland and Ukraine and was killed on 8 June 1919 when the fabric covering the wing of his old SPAD VII tore loose and the aircraft crashed.

Jasta 62

The star of *Jasta* 62 – and its youthful leader – was Ltn d R Max Näther. Born in Tepliwoda, East Prussia, in August 1899, he emerged as one of the youngest German aces. Still only 15 when he joined the army in 1914, Näther was twice wounded and then commissioned in 1916. Transferring to the aviation service, he bypassed the two-seater route and went directly to *Jasta* 62 in March 1918. His first kill came on 16 May, and by 22 July he was not only CO of the *Jasta* – at 18 – but had 11 victories. Näther may not have flown the D VII until after his return from leave in late August.

He took his score to 26 – out of a unit total of 49 – by the end of the war. Like several others, Näther's nomination for the 'Blue Max' failed to be confirmed before the collapse. And, like a number of D VII aces, he survived the war, only to die in later conflicts. Näther participated in Germany's border war with Poland, being downed over Kolmar on 8 January 1919 by ground fire.

Jasta 68

The founding CO of *Jasta* 68 was Ltn Fritz Pütter, who was born in the Westphalian town of Duelmen on 14 January 1895. He first saw army service on the Eastern Front, where his courage earned him a commission and a transfer to the 370th Infantry Regiment in October 1915. Volunteering for the aviation service in May 1916, Pütter eventually went to *Jasta* 9 in March 1917, where he gained ten victories by the end of January 1918. The next month he took command of *Jasta* 68, and by May his tally stood at 25 kills. This earned him the 'Blue Max' and some leave.

One of the youngest German aces was Max Näther, who went off to war as a 15-year-old in 1914. Promoted to Leutnant der Reserve when still 16, he would be appointed CO of *Jasta* 62 in July 1918. His score reached 25 on 29 October – the same day he was recommended for the 'Blue Max'. Like other D VII aces whose tallies reached this crucial mark too late, Näther never actually received the award *(Franks collection)*

Fritz Pütter fell victim to unstable phosphorus ammunition self-igniting in the summer heat of 1918. On 16 July he landed his burning D VII on the *Jasta* 68 airfield but was badly injured. He died in hospital on 10 August. Pütter's *Pour le Mérite* had been awarded on 31 May 1918, and he attained a score of 25 kills

Wilhelm Stör of *Jasta* 68 appears to be missing out on the fun as he sits in his D VII while other *Staffel* pilots do their best to entertain visiting nurses. 'Willy' Stör achieved five victories in 1918. His Fokker-built D VII displays a white winged sword personal marking on its four-colour fabric, and the fighter would have also shown the *Jasta* marking of a broad black and white band on the aft fuselage *(A Imrie via HAC/UTD)*

Returning to his command on 14 July, Pütter was seriously injured two days later when he fell victim to the premature ignition of phosphorus ammunition, which set his new D VII ablaze. The 23-year-old was badly burned and he died on 10 August.

His replacement was Ltn Rudolf Otto, who had likewise flown two-seaters prior to joining *Jasta* 74 (where he claimed three kills). Tranferring to *Jasta* 68, he became an ace with the D VII by claiming three further victories confirmed and a fourth unconfirmed. Wilhelm Stör also scored five victories with the *Jasta*, two of which were balloons.

Jasta 72s

Saxon *Jasta* 72 had received 12 D VIIs by July, former *Jasta* 3 ace Oblt d R Karl Menckhoff being the unit's founding *Staffelführer*. Older than most of his comrades at 35, he was a Westphalian from Herford, born on 14 April 1883. Menckhoff started military service in 1903, but an appendicitis operation cut short his career. Upon the outbreak of war, however, he was accepted into the infantry, decorated and wounded, all by the end of 1914.

Transferring to the air service, he flew on the Eastern Front, then became an instructor and, finally, as an NCO, was posted to *Jasta* 3 in early 1917. His first victory came on 5 April, and a year later he had 20 victories, having been wounded along the way. On 23 April 1918 Menckhoff received the *Pour le Mérite,* raising his score to 25. In February he became CO of *Jasta* 72. During May, June and July his score rose inexorably, reaching 39, but on the evening of 25 July he was downed near Château-Thierry by 1Lt Walter Avery of the US 95th Aero Squadron and taken prisoner.

Menckhoff's D VII carried a large letter 'M' on the fuselage, which Walter Avery cut off as a souvenir. Avery had already been awarded the French *Croix de Guerre* for his work with the French *Escadrille* 471, but this was his first action with the 95th. In his history of the unit, Harold Buckley wrote;

'Avery, who had been in the squadron but two days, burst into fame in a most spectacular manner by bring-

Ten Fokker-built D VIIs of Saxon *Jasta* 72 show off their individual insignia in this line-up on Bergnicourt aerodrome, near Rethel, in July 1918. First in line is the distinctive 'M'-marked machine of *Staffelführer* Karl Menckhoff, and third is Gustav Frädrich's 383/18, adorned with a black-bordered white diagonal stripe. On both these aircraft the individual emblem is repeated on the top wing. Also evident is the modification of the wing crosses from the initial wide, fully-bordered format, the insignia change apparently being achieved by the painting of crude 'lozenges' over the edges in imitation of the printed camouflage fabric

Karl Menckhoff had scored 39 victories by 25 July 1918, but his career came to an end that same day when he was brought down behind French lines by Walter Avery of the US 95th Aero Squadron on his very first patrol with the unit. Menckhoff gave a distinctly haughty impression to his Allied captors, and was reportedly chagrined when he learned his adversary was an American tyro rather than a famous French ace. Avery took the 'M' insignia from the D VII as a trophy, but was chided for refusing to take the German ace's 'Blue Max' and other decorations.

This fine study of Gustav Frädrich of *Jasta* 72 provides details of the way the early German parachute system worked. Frädrich adjusts his Heinecke harness as the mechanic holds the parachute pack, which acted as a seat cushion and went with the pilot when he jumped clear of the aircraft. The 'chute was opened by a static line, if all went well. Pilots such as Udet, Bäumer, Osterkamp and Raesch saved their lives with successful jumps, but several others died when their 'chutes failed to deploy correctly. Frädrich's D VII 383/18 displays his personal emblem on the fuselage side and top

This time unencumbered by his parachute, Frädrich of Saxon *Jasta* 72 strikes a jaunty pose with his well-worn D VII 383/18. This Fokker-built aircraft has a replacement starboard wheel from an OAW machine and a rack for flares attached to the cockpit side. On the original print the personal marking can be discerned on the top of the fuselage and also the upper wing. Also noteworthy is the (possibly) hand-painted 'lozenge' pattern around the fuselage cross, effected during conversion of the national insignia

ing down Baron Menckhoff, a famous German ace of 39 victories. For Avery, it was the first. Menckhoff was brought down alive, and he immediately asked to meet the man who had out-manoeuvred him and fought so superbly. When told it was a new American pilot he was much chagrined, having already decided in his own mind that it was Fonck or some equally celebrated Allied ace.'

Menckhoff was still a prisoner in October 1919, but escaped from France into Switzerland, where he decided to stay. There, he became a businessman, and died in 1948.

Ltn d R Herbert Mahn arrived at *Jasta* 72 on 3 June 1918, and he soon scored against the French. By the end of the war he had destroyed eight SPADs and a balloon.

Ltn d R Gustav Frädrich had seen early service in Macedonia with Fl. Abt. 30, being credited with his first kill in May 1917. He also flew with *Jastas* 1 and 39, but without success in air combat. In March 1918 Frädrich moved to *Jasta* 72, and between 25 July and 18 October he claimed five more victories over French aircraft. He took command of the *Jasta* on 23 October.

Jasta 73

Ltn Fritz Gerhard Anders was CO of *Jasta* 73 in the summer of 1918. He had in fact learned to fly pre-war, gaining a licence in 1912 and having

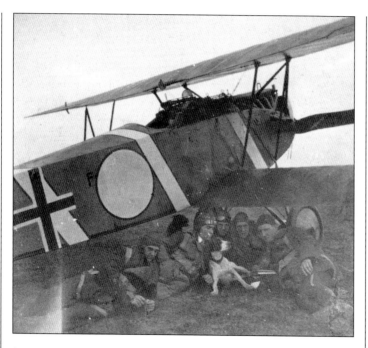

been on active duty for most of the conflict, except while recovering from wounds. Anders, who had flown with both *Jasta* 35b and *Jasta* 4 (he scored his first victory with the latter unit), became leader of *Jasta* 73 on 20 February 1918.

Jasta 73 was a premier nightfighter unit, flying nocturnal intercept missions against French Voisin bombers. Fritz Anders made a number of night interceptions, most likely in a D VII, scoring five night victories in August and September, taking his score to seven overall. Ltn Franz Kirchfeld was the *Jasta's* top scorer with eight victories (two at night) and two unconfirmed claims. The last six were all accounted for in September and October, so these were probably most claimed with a D VII.

Jasta 74

Leader of *Jasta* 74, Oblt Theodor Cammann achieved a victory prior to joining *Jasta* Boelcke as acting *Staffelführer* in January 1918. With another kill under his belt, he moved to *Jasta* 74 on 21 February, taking command about a month later. By 27 June Cammann had claimed eight

Jasta 73 ace Ltn d R Fritz Jacobsen is generally credited with five to eight victories, although in his later years he claimed he had scored twelve kills. He appears in this photo with his own D VII, named *Schnuck*. Jacobsen lived until 1981, and was helpful to many aviation historians *(Dr D H M Gröschel)*

Jasta 73 pioneered the development of nocturnal air fighting, claiming several French night bombers. On 21/22 August 1918, *Staffel* CO Fritz Anders brought down this Voisin 10 No 2995 to score his fourth victory, having downed two aircraft the previous night. The crew of MdL Anot and MdL Roberini of *Escadrille* V 116 were taken prisoner *(A Imrie via HAC/UTD)*

victories, and he had increased this to twelve with the D VII by war's end.

Wilhelm 'Willy' Hippert was already a seven-kill ace with *Jasta* 39 when he arrived at the unit from Italy in the early summer of 1918. The NCO pilot gained his eighth, and final, kill with a D VII, plus another unconfirmed. *Jasta* 74 only achieved 24 victories in the war.

This BMW-powered D VIIF 505/18 of Vzfw 'Willy' Hippert of *Jasta* 74 is one of the rare authentic examples of a true 'chequerboard Fokker' as often mentioned in Allied reports. The *Jasta* marking was reported to have been a dark blue nose, and the black and white pattern represents a personal embellishment. The wheel covers may have also been painted blue, with four small equi-distant markings. The name *Mimmi*. is displayed on the upper wing. The upper cowling panel has supplementary cooling holes

3rd ARMY – *JAGDGRUPPE Nr* 11

From mid-May 1918 *Jagdgruppe Nr* 11 comprised *Jastas* 17, 48, 53 and 61. Although it served mostly with the 3rd Army along the Reims Front, the unit also saw action with both the 9th Army (25 July to 18 September) and the 7th Army (18-25 September). The unit CO from its formation through to war's end was Rittmeister Heinz von Brederlow, who was another seasoned commander rather than a fighter ace.

Jasta 17

Julius Buckler was the outstanding *Jasta* 17 ace. Born in Mainz on 28 March 1894, he was yet another airman to rise from humble working-class origins (his father was a roofer) to achieve national fame through military achievements. After working as a roofer himself, Buckler enlisted in a Hessian infantry regiment and saw action in France when war broke out. He was wounded on the Marne in September 1914, forcing him to transfer to the aviation service. Upon being rated a pilot, Buckler joined *Artillerie Flieger Abteilung* 209 on the Verdun front and served with the unit for over a year. He transferred to newly-formed *Jasta* 17 in late 1916.

Over the next year Buckler scored 30 victories, although he was wounded four more times. On 29 November 1917, he was hit in the back and arms and crashed in no-man's land. After lying beneath the wreck of his aircraft for many hours, he was finally rescued by counter-attacking

German infantry. Having already been commissioned, Buckler received the 'Blue Max' on 3 December 1917, the medal being presented to him by Gen von der Marwitz as Buckler lay in his hospital bed. The ace returned only to be shot down and wounded again – for the fifth time – on 6 May 1918, thus winning him the dubious honour of the Wound Badge in Gold.

Once back at *Jasta* 17 (probably in August) Buckler became, by his own account, *Staffelführer* after the wounding of Ltn Günther Schuster. Some historians doubt Buckler was the official CO, although he

Jasta 74's Willy Hippert demonstrates the use of oxygen equipment for high altitudes. The oxygen flowed from the metal canister affixed to the fuselage into the hand-controlled rubber bladder and then to a pipe stem in the pilot's mouth

certainly led the *Jasta* in the air. His last few claims were scored in the D VII, which brought his tally to 36 official victories with, according to his records, another seven unconfirmed. His primary aircraft was always named *Mops*, and late in the war he had a reserve machine called *Lily*. He was commissioned as a major in the Luftwaffe in the 1930s and died in Berlin in May 1960.

Christian Friedrich Donhauser had flown two-seaters with Fl. Abt. 10 before becoming a fighter pilot, having gained one (possibly unconfirmed) victory with his observer in May 1918. Posted to *Jasta* 17 in July 1918, he soon made his mark as a solid NCO pilot. By the end of the war Donhauser had scored 15 official kills (*Jasta* 17 records state 19) and been awarded the Golden Military Merit Cross on 9 October.

Commissioned into the Reichswehr after the war, he turned up at Koblenz in 1919 test flying German fighters for the Allies. The German Aeroplane Delivery Committee was handing over aircraft to the American occupation forces in Koblenz, as specified under the Armistice terms. Wary of sabotage, the Americans insisted that each machine be test flown by a German airman, and Donhauser was one such pilot. He became quite well known to the Americans at Koblenz, but died in the fiery crash of one of the Fokkers he was testing.

Ltn d R Alfred Fleischer came from Silesia and served with a grenadier regiment in 1914. He saw action at Verdun and on the Somme before being wounded in the second half of 1916. After transferring to the aviation service, he flew with *Jasta* 17 in 1918 and scored six victories (five with the D VII). Fleischer's second victory, but his first on a D VII, came on 1 August when he downed a 27th Aero Squadron Nieuport 28.

It turned out to be a black day for the unit's pilots, who were escorting a Salmson photographic two-seater. Attacked by Fokkers of JG I, three Nieuports were shot down, plus the Salmson. Lt M Clifford McElvain managed to break away and head for home, but stumbled onto *Jasta* 17, led by its commander, Ltn Günther Schuster. Later, Fleischer recorded;

'From our base at Balàtre we advanced directly to the front, and had almost reached an altitude of 14,000 ft when something very surprising occurred. Suddenly, and entirely unnoticed by all of us probably coming directly from the sun,

Julius Buckler scored all his 36 victories while serving with *Jasta* 17. He flew with the unit from its formation to the end of the war, being commissioned on 18 November 1917 and receiving the 'Blue Max' the following 4 December. He probably scored his final three victories, and made an unconfirmed claim, on 8 November 1918 in a D VII. His boyish face shows little evidence of over three years of war service and several serious wounds *(HAC/UTD)*

From 10 June to 1 August 1918, *Jasta* 17 was led by Ltn d R Günther Schuster, who claimed six confirmed victories, the last with the D VII on 15 July. As commander, he marked his D VII (Alb) with a completely (possibly) black fuselage and a white lightning bolt. Schuster was wounded on 1 August by Lt McElvain of the 27th Aero Squadron, who was brought down by Alfred Fleischer soon afterwards

A smiling Christian Donhauser displays a '17' arm patch signifying the *Jasta* to which he belongs, together with his Albatros-built Fokker D VII. The white radiator shell formed part of the *Jagdstaffel* 17 unit marking *(N W O'Connor)*

a small enemy biplane of unknown type dashed with lightning speed upon our leader's 'plane and opened fire at close range. An abrupt and instinctive glance over my shoulder assured me that at the moment there was no danger for me. My back was clear. Therefore, eyes front and aid my hard-pressed comrade, who had already been disabled and been forced to bring his smoking 'plane down in a sudden dive.

'I immediately directed the fire of my two guns at our adversary,

Alfred Fleischer of *Jasta* 17 is seen in his D VII (Alb). The nose is black with a white radiator shell. The colour of the personal marking on the five-colour fabric is unrecorded, but it is probably yellow

thereby forcing him away from my comrade. In order to escape my deadly barrage, my adversary climbed steeply so that he stood almost perpendicularly above me. This manoeuvre to gain safe altitude would have been achieved by him if my brave Fokker had not shown an unusually marvellous performance. In great style it followed this dash for altitude and hung onto its propeller so that I could cover my adversary with a well-directed, and continuous, fire. In full recognition of this great danger the enemy pilot allowed his 'plane to glide down over the left wing, and in this manner escaped my fire. By this manoeuvre he reached approximately the same altitude, and now the advantages of my Fokker were demonstrated.

'Persistently and with resolute determination, the pilot attempted to fight me off again and again. Closely together we circled around each other. How long this circular battle continued I don't know. At an altitude of approximately 1000 to 1500 ft, I was successful, after having completed a reverse ascending curve, to place several well directed shots. Soon thereafter I was able to gain a position 120 to 150 ft behind him, and had already aimed my machine guns upon him ready to pull the trigger in the fever of the chase. Then I saw that the propeller of my adversary stood still and then the 'plane, completely out of control, prepared to land.

'A few minutes later the Nieuport crashed into a small wooded spot and the pilot climbed out of the wreckage and waved to me above, probably with mixed feelings. I found a suitable place to land then went over to the pilot who, rather fatigued though smiling, stepped forward towards me. Like two good old friends we shook hands and smiled like two boys after a successfully completed adventure.'

Albatros-built Fokkers of *Jasta* 17 await their pilots on a bright summer day. Most display the unit's black and white noses, with personal insignia generally applied between the cockpit and fuselage cross. At the far end is *Staffelführer* Schuster's lightning bolt-decorated machine *(Justin Young)*

Clifford McElvain recorded his own view of this event some years later;

'The observation 'plane had gone. My flight had gone. I had had enough for one day and I headed for home. As I flew I discovered too late that I was on a collision course with a flight of five Fokker D VIIs, coming at them out of the sun, and they apparently did not see me. At the moment it seemed to me that it was too late for me to do anything but open fire, and my first burst went into one. I couldn't watch to see what happened to him, but I learned later from Fleischer that he was wounded and crashed, but survived (Ltn Schuster). The three others simply got out of the way and circled, leaving one man to deal with me by himself.

'I was very light in both fuel and ammunition, so my Nieuport was especially agile. Fleischer's Fokker D VII was faster and could out-climb me. His Fokker was "supercharged" (had a high-compression engine), and at 13,000 ft his supercharger gave him considerable advantage in climb and speed, but even so our 'planes were pretty well matched. Each had its own superior characteristics – he could out-climb and out-dive me and I could make tighter turns.

'Fleischer later admitted I put a few holes in his 'plane and he scattered some splinters over me when one of his bullets hit a wooden longeron in my fuselage, but no real damage was done to either. Then, without any warning, my engine suddenly "blooped" and died, and there I was in combat without power, losing altitude fast. My propeller continued to windmill and my guns would still fire, but all I could do was spar as best I could as he chased me right down to the ground. I sat waiting for the crash ahead, and at the same time expecting the bullets from behind that would keep me from feeling it. It was only when I slowed down for the crash that my propeller stopped. In that instant the Fokker dived past me and the pilot waved. He had seen my propeller stop and knew I was through.'

The two men met again after World War 2 when Fleischer's family was struggling to survive in post-war West Germany. Fleischer contacted McElvain, who helped him and his family move to the USA by acting as

1 August 1918 was a bad day for the US 27th Aero Squadron, the unit losing four Nieuport 28s in combat. Lt Clifford McElvain, second from right, was brought down by *Jasta* 17's Fleischer and taken prisoner. Remarkably, this event started a friendship between the two men and their families which lasted over 45 years

Five *Jagdstaffel* 53 pilots appear ready for flight in front of their Albatros-built D VIIs, which display the white nose unit markings and individually coloured tail sections. They are, from left to right, Vzfw Friedrich Poeschke (the unit's top scorer with eight victories), Ltn Franz Freitag, Gefr Hugo Dressler, Vzfw Hermann Korsch (the two-victory pilot known as *der Kleine Korsch*, 'the little Korsch') and Gefr Gönnheimer *(HAC/UTD)*

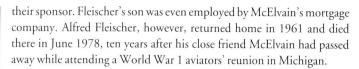

Wilhelm Frickart achieved his first victories as an observer on the Eastern Front in 1917. He went on to fly with *Jasta* 65, taking his tally to 12 by war's end

On 3 October 1918 Hans Marwede of *Jasta* 67 attacked a balloon of the US 6th Balloon Company and set it ablaze after two or three passes. Marwede was, however, immediately forced down by machine gun fire from the ground, his D VII (OAW) overturning on landing. Hundreds of 'doughboys' quickly converged on the site and the Fokker was soon stripped for souvenirs

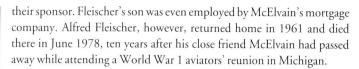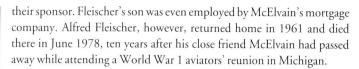

their sponsor. Fleischer's son was even employed by McElvain's mortgage company. Alfred Fleischer, however, returned home in 1961 and died there in June 1978, ten years after his close friend McElvain had passed away while attending a World War 1 aviators' reunion in Michigan.

Jasta 53

Oblt Robert Hildebrandt of *Jasta* 69 transferred to command *Jasta* 53 in late October 1918. He was already an ace with *Jastas* 13 and 12, but would only add one D VII victory to his score with *Jasta* 53. The top scorer was Vzfw Friedrich Poeschke, who had arrived on 5 May 1918. By the time the D VIIs started arriving, he probably had one victory to his name, but by 2 November he had added seven more.

Jasta 61

Siegfried Büttner came to *Jasta* 61 from *Jasta* 22 on 7 June 1918, having already scored four victories. His fifth victory was probably downed in a D VII on 9 August, and before the month was out his tally had rocketed to 13, including seven balloons.

3rd ARMY — JAGDGRUPPE Nr 9

Jagdgruppe Nr 9 apparently comprised *Jagdstaffeln* 3, 47w, 49, 54s and 77b within the 3rd Army between 9 July and 8 September. As aces from *Jastas* 3, 54s and 77b are covered elsewhere, only those of 47w and 49 are mentioned here. *Gruppe* CO was Oblt Hermann Kohze, who was *Staffelführer* of *Jasta* 3 from April 1917 until 4 September 1918. Previously with KG 4, he spent various periods in charge of JGr 9 between February and July 1918 during its time with the 4th and 2nd armies.

Jasta 47w

Württemberg *Jasta* 47 certainly had D VIIs on strength in the last months of the war, but it appears to have seen little action, if only because few victories were claimed. Vzfw Friedrich Ehmann was its leading light, although his score is unclear. Generally noted as having six kills by the end of May 1918, the ex-*Kest* 5 pilot's actions after this date are only glimpsed via other records, although it seems that he scored twice more – once in July and, finally, on 4 November in a D VII. His report requesting confirmation and credit of this kill is dated 5 November, and says in part;

'Fokker D VII 4508/18, fuselage nose red, fuselage back from the nose brown, with a yellow ring. Report – On 4 November 1918 I flew to the front with a group of five Fokker machines. At 1530 hrs I saw five enemy bombers coming from the direction of Sedan. At a height of 3500 m I managed to attack them. After a short series of bursts, the two-seater SPAD machine dived down, leaving behind a thick cloud of smoke, north of Touly. I observed its fall to about

The disheartened Hans Marwede of *Jasta* 67 sits forlornly under guard by an American soldier after being shot down. Adding insult to injury, his capture had been filmed by the US Signal Corps

700 m. It is lying on this side of the lines. Type – SPAD two-seater.'

The only recorded French casualties are Cpls Clauzel and Herbault of an unknown SPAD unit, who were both reported missing.

Jasta 49

One *Jasta* 49 pilot who may have achieved significant victories on the D VII was Ltn d R Hermann Habich. Born in Bühl in August 1895 and taught to fly pre-war, he saw action with a two-seater unit on the Eastern Front and, requesting a transfer to a fighter unit, he eventually reached *Jasta* 49 in January 1918. Habich gained one victory in March and six more in September and October. After the war he remained in aviation, and in World War 2 served with the Luftwaffe, commanding a *Nachtschlachtgruppe* on the Eastern Front.

ARMY GROUP 'C' – JAGDGRUPPE SIEMPELKAMP

Formed from *Jastas* 64w and 65, *Jagdgruppe* Siempelkamp was commanded by Ltn Eugen Siempelkamp, who had previously been with *Jastas* 4 and 29 and led *Jasta* 64w from July 1918. He became an ace in September by scoring two victories but was wounded on the 14th. The formation then became *Jagdgruppe* Marville and was transferred to the neighbouring 5th Army sector under the leadership of Ltn Julius Fichter, who was *Jasta* 67 *Staffelführer*. *Staffel* 64w was dropped from the new formation, leaving *Jasta* 65 to combine with *Jasta* 67.

Jasta 65

Otto Fritzner led *Jasta* 65 after service with *Jasta* 17 in 1917-18. He ended the war with nine victories, of which three being possibly scored with the D VII. Ltn der Landwehr Wilhelm Frickart, who had flown two-seaters on the Eastern Front in 1917 as an observer, became a pilot and joined *Jasta* 64w in mid-1918, before moving to *Jasta* 65 on 19 August. Most of his 12 kills were achieved as an observer, and only his last four came in the Fokker fighter.

Jasta 67

Hans Marwede is led away for interrogation by US troops. His face was either bloodied during the crash landing or perhaps as a result of some rough handling by his captors

Uffz Hans Heinrich Marwede was a former *Kest* pilot who was assigned to *Jasta* 67 in June 1918. Between then and 3 October he accounted for one DH 9 and four observation balloons, three of the latter falling during the course of a late afternoon sortie on 14 September. He was captured after his fifth victory on 3 October when his D VII was hit by ground fire from the American 6th Balloon Company. The whole episode was recorded on film by US Signal Corps photographers, and Marwede ended up under American guard, bruised and dejected.

He later rose to high rank in the Luftwaffe, but Marwede lost his killed in a flying accident before World War 2.

DEFENDING THE FATHERLAND

On 6 June 1918 the British War Cabinet created the Independent Air Force (IAF) of the RAF. Commanded by Maj Gen Sir H M Trenchard, it was charged with carrying out a programme of strategic bombing of industrial and railway targets in south-western Germany. Its daylight bombing units included Nos 55 (DH 4s), 99 and 104 (DH 9s) Sqns. Based at Azelot, south of Nancy, the valiant IAF airmen would make many raids deep into enemy territory against targets such as Thionville, Metz, Saarbrücken, Mannheim and Cologne.

They were opposed by the fighters of the home defence *Kampfeinsitzer Staffeln* or *Kests,* which were equipped with a variety of aircraft and based throughout the region in 1918. Unfortunately for the IAF crews, they would also cross the territory of the *Jastas* of the 19th Army near Metz, especially *Jagdgruppe Nr 9*, which from 8 September comprised *Jastas* 3, 18, 54s, 77b and 80b, as well as *Kest* 3. Besides taking a heavy toll of the IAF bombers, these units also frequently encountered French and American squadrons from the sector around Toul and Nancy. Between the 19th Army sector and the Swiss border were Army Group 'A' and Army Group 'B'. The *Jastas* and *Kests* in these areas produced few D VII aces.

19th ARMY – *JAGDGRUPPE Nr 9*

Jagdgruppe 9 was led by *Jasta* 18's CO, Ltn d R August Raben. Born on 2 December 1892, Raben had been promoted to leutnant while serving with *2 Thüringisches Feldartillerie Regiment Nr 55* in December 1914. In April 1916 he transferred to the aviation service and flew with *Kampfgeschwader 5/Schutzstaffel 7* until January 1917, when he moved to *Jasta* 36. Remaining with the unit until the beginning of August, Raben then went to Italy, where he gained two victories as CO of *Jasta* 39.

In March 1918 he was appointed CO of *Jasta* 15 in France, and when this unit became part of an exchange arrangement with *Jasta* 18 (see below), he took over *Jagdstaffel* 18, but was injured in a crash on 20 March. Raben returned on 14 April and scored another two victories over IAF bombers in August. On the 21st he took command of *Jagdgruppe* Raben (JGr 9) until war's end. Although he finished the conflict with just four victories, this highly decorated veteran had proved himself to be an extremely capable and inspiring leader.

When Rudolf Berthold became JG II CO in March 1918, he wanted to have his old unit (*Jasta* 18) as part of his new command. This could only be achieved by exchanging the personnel of *Jasta* 15 for those of *Jasta* 18, Berthold therefore getting his men but not the *Jasta* number. This meant that JG II retained its original *Jastas* – 12, 13, 15 and 19 – but with the ex-*Jasta* 18 pilots now operating as *Jasta* 15.

Jasta 3 represented part of the German opposition to the raids of the Independent Air Force. *Staffelfüher* Georg Weiner flew this Albatros-built D VII, which displays his initial. A gunsight is mounted between the Spandaus, and note that the lower starboard wing seems to have been over-painted in an unknown colour

Jasta 3

Ltn Georg Weiner emerged as *Jasta* 3's sole ace at this stage of the war. He, like Raben, was a *Schutzstaffel* pilot prior to moving to *Jasta* 20, where he gained his first victory in March 1917. Weiner then transferred to *Kest* 3, where he claimed two French SPADs and an IAF bomber before being appointed *Jasta* 3 CO in early September 1918. Flying his Albatros-built D VII marked with a large 'W' on the fuselage, he added five more scalps to his tally to give him a final total of nine. Weiner's *Kest* 3 victory of 16 September 1918 was over the DH 4 piloted by Lt W E Johns of No 55 Sqn, who later gained fame as the creator of fictional hero *Biggles*.

Jasta 18

Staffel Raben had begun to receive D VIIs by June 1918 whilst still located at Lomme and attached to 6th Army. As 'Raben' translates as

The 'Ravens' of *Jasta* 18 form a proud group before their *Starthaus* or ready shack, which was painted in the unit's red and white colours with the famous Raben emblem in various hues. They are, from left to right, Glatz (one victory), Wilhelm Kühne (seven), Hans Müller (13), Kurt Monnington (eight), *Staffelführer* August Raben (four), Erich Spindler (two), Kurt Baier (one), Heinz Küstner (two) and Kandt

'ravens', a black raven emblem was applied to the fuselages of the unit's aircraft. The Fokkers were painted with red noses and wings and white rear fuselages and tails, with personal markings also being added to fuselages or tails. As *Staffelführer,* Raben distinguished his D VII with a greater display of red, together with a white raven. By mid-June *Jasta* 18 was based at Montingen (Montoy), east of Metz, making it ideally placed to intercept IAF bomber formations. The 'Ravens' became adept at breaking up the ranks of de Havilland bombers and

Wilhelm Kühne and his loyal groundcrew are photographed with an Albatros-built D VII of *Jasta* 18 in the summer of 1918. The vermilion wings and nose, as well as the raven emblem stencilled on the fuselage, are all in evidence

then picking off the stragglers. *Jasta* 18 also had its share of battles with American aircraft too, especially the SPADs of the 13th Aero Squadron.

Ltn d R Kurt Monnington had been in the army before pilot training, and he initially flew two-seaters in Fl. Abt. 62. As a *jagdflieger,* he first joined *Jasta* 15 and then, following the mass transfer, flew with *Jasta* 18. Monnington had scored his initial kill against an SE 5 on 11 May 1918, and he followed it up with victory over a Bristol F2B on 5 June. Then came the move south to the 19th Army, after which he went on to shoot down six IAF de Havilland bombers before the war ran its course. Two of these bombers represented a 'double' on 13 August, when a DH9 he was attacking collided with another.

Offz Stv Wilhelm Kühne scored seven victories, plus six more unconfirmed or claims lost through arbitration – there were no shared kills in the German Air Service, and if two or more pilots claimed the same one, a third party decided who should receive the credit. Kühne was born on 11 December 1888 and enlisted in a fusilier regiment in 1909. A pre-war airman, he transferred to the air arm in 1913 and flew two-seaters with Fl. Abt. 14. After training in a *Jastaschule,* he went to *Jasta* 29 in February 1917 and then joined *Jasta* 15 in January 1918, moving to *Jasta* 18 in the personnel exchange.

Kühne's initial confirmed victory was attained on 25 March 1918, but it took him until early August to move his total to five. Two more confirmed kills in late August brought his score to seven (including four balloons) before his death in action against IAF bombers on 30 August. Kühne had seen his *Staffelführer* Raben in a dangerous situation during the *Jasta* attack on a superior number of DH 9s and gone to his aid. Raben escaped but Kühne fell to the gunners of No 55 Sqn.

The flamboyant Fokkers of *Staffel* Raben on parade at Möntingen. First in line is the D VII of CO Ltn Raben, distinguished by a mostly red fuselage and a white raven. These 11 red and white aircraft must have made a dazzling sight, whether in the air or on the ground

One of the deadliest of the 'Ravens' was Ltn d R Hans Müller, who was born in Etzel, Friesland, on 3 July 1896. Joining the infantry in April 1914, he transferred to aviation, and two-seaters, in 1916. Müller briefly flew Triplanes with

Jasta 15 in early 1918, gaining three victories before the pilot swap. By the time the D VIIs started to arrive he had five victories, and he ended the war with 12 confirmed claims, scored against the RAF, the French and the US Air Service.

14 September 1918 – the third day of the St Mihiel offensive – would be a proud day for the Raben *Staffel*. It would also bring an ordeal for the 13th Aero Squadron. A patrol of 'Grim Reaper' SPADs was bounced by the red and white Fokkers at about 0900 hrs, Müller, Ltn Günther von Büren and Ltn Heinz Küstner all subsequently claiming victories. 1Lt Leighton Brewer of the 13th vividly recalled the combat many years later;

'On the 14th we were given a low patrol – 2500 m – and we were flying this when we were attacked by a bunch of red-nosed Fokkers. We lost four 'planes within one minute! The first indication that I had of the thing was seeing a red Fokker with a white fuselage, standing on its nose and spraying the fellow in the back of me with bullets. Two Fokkers with red wings and noses and white fuselages came down on us and they shot down the men on each side of me. Charlie Drew, George Kull, "Buck" Freeman and "Steve" Brody were all lost. Drew was very badly wounded, Kull was killed and the other two were prisoners.'

1Lt Charles Drew had barely survived. He later reported;

'I flew No 2 position in the first flight of a squadron patrol of three flights, Maj Charles J Biddle, CO, leading. At approximately 0903 hrs I observed three Fokker biplanes dive through our first flight, partially breaking up the formation. Two of our 'planes went down with the last Fokker and were apparently in trouble, so I dove from my position at the right rear of the formation, and at an altitude of about 2000 m engaged the enemy 'plane nose-on at a range of about 150 m, receiving an incendiary bullet in my right thigh, which partially paralysed my right leg. I continued the fight, although greatly handicapped by my loss in speed and inability to use my right leg. I received several direct bursts, one bullet ripping my blouse open and another my breeches. Finally, at about 0920 hrs, I was hit in the right arm by an explosive bullet.'

At this point Drew fainted, but revived in time to bring his aircraft down to a crash-landing behind German lines. He went on;

'The enemy 'plane was painted a brilliant scarlet on the upper and lower wing, engine housing and three-quarters of the way back along the fuselage, while the tail sections were striped black and white.'

Drew was taken prisoner and his right arm was amputated in a German hospital.

1Lt Freeman later said that his aircraft came down due to engine failure, but three of the SPADs were credited to Müller and another went to von Büren before he, in turn, was wounded by the Americans. Brody's SPAD wound up as a trophy on the *jasta* airfield. Later that afternoon Müller claimed another SPAD (apparently from SPA 153) for his

With his perky pup close at hand, Günther von Büren of *Jasta* 18 is seen with his distinctively-marked D VII. The raven emblem was augmented by four running chicks. Note the flare pistol fitted to the upper wing centre section and the cooling holes cut into the cowling – both common features of aircraft serving with this *Staffel*. Büren claimed an IAF bomber and an American SPAD destroyed

A grim personal insignia identifies the OAW-built D VII of Saxon *Jasta* 54's Erich Mix. Seen here with his mechanic, Mix holds an *Abschuss Stock* or victory stick. The two white stripes indicate that this photograph was taken after his second claim on 3 September 1918

fourth of the day, one of which had represented the unit's 100th victory. On 1 October the 13th Aero Squadron met *Staffel* Raben again and lost two pilots to Müller and Küstner.

Jasta 54s

Saxon *Jasta* 54 only achieved 22 victories by war's end, but one of its more interesting pilots was Uffz Erich Mix. He may have gained two or all of his three World War 1 kills with a D VII (plus one unconfirmed balloon) before finally becoming an ace in World War 2. An ex-infantryman, Mix came to *Jasta* 54 in June 1918 and was commissioned after the war. Serving with the Luftwaffe in the 1930s, by 1939 he was technical officer of I./JG 53. Mix later became CO of III./JG 2, and by the end of 1939 he had become an ace, with kills in both wars. He subsequently saw action during the battles of France and Britain, and his last claim (a Blenheim west of Den Haag) was made in 1941, taking Mix's overall score to 11.

Jasta 77b

Bavarian Jasta 77 may not have had many D VIIs during the war's final months. It was commanded by Ltn Max Gossner from 16 July until the Armistice. A Bavarian from Weilheim, Gossner was born on 25 August 1894 and was serving with a Bavarian infantry regiment upon the outbreak of war. He was wounded on 12 August 1914, commissioned a year later and transferred to the aviation service in March 1916. Gossner arrived at *Jasta* 23b in September 1917, where he befriended 'Fritz' Röth. Gaining two victories with this unit, he then followed Röth to *Jasta* 16b, serving there until appointed CO of *Jasta* 77b in July 1918. Gossner's last six victories – which included two American balloons on 15 September – were most likely scored with a D VII.

Offz Stv Bernhard Ultsch was the only other *Jasta* ace. Another Bavarian, he was born on 26 March 1898 in Wunseidel, and initially saw action with the artillery before transferring to aviation in September 1916. Ultsch's first unit was *Schutzstaffel* 29 and, together with his observer, he gained three confirmed claims in 1917 prior to moving to *Jasta* 39 in Italy. Five victories scored while serving with this unit, including three Caproni bombers, took his total to eight.

Back in France, and now wearing the Bavarian Military Merit Cross 3rd Class with Swords, the Iron Cross 1st Class and the Austrian Silver Bravery Medal 2nd Class, Ultsch joined *Jasta* 77b in February 1918. Two confirmed and two unconfirmed claims came in March, but he was wounded in May. By the time he returned in August the unit had D VIIs. Ultsch's final two kills were gained in September 1918, as was his last decoration, the Bavarian Military Merit Cross 2nd Class with Swords.

Jasta 80b

Jasta 80b was probably equipped with D VIIs by September 1918, by which time its CO was Oblt Erwin Wenig, who gained his fourth, and last, victory with a Fokker that same month.

Former engineer and regular army officer Ltn Kurt Seit came to the unit in June 1918, just before his 24th birthday. He gained five victories before war's end, the last three possibly with a D VII. Seit was wounded four times during the conflict and held the Silver Wound Badge. A sixth victory was claimed, but the credit went to another pilot.

Oblt Gottlieb Rassberger gained four victories with the *Staffel*, which he had joined in March 1918

Kest 3

Other than Georg Weiner who, as previously noted, claimed three kills prior to the D VII's arrival, *Kest* 3 boasted no aces. The unit probably continued to operate a mix of types in the war's final weeks and, in any case, scored only thee victories during the D VII period.

THE BITTER END

Severely hampered by a lack of fuel and replacements, *Jagdstaffel* pilots fought on as best they could against an ever-growing tide of Allied aircraft. Although in most cases their fighting spirit remained unbroken, they were usually unable to prevent the superior number of enemy airmen from accomplishing their missions. Then came 11 November 1918.

When orders arrived to lay down their arms and deliver their beloved Fokkers to the Allies, the *Jasta* airmen were shocked and embittered. Worse still, they would return to a Germany torn by revolution, with military discipline in complete disintegration. Alfred Fleischer of *Jasta* 17 was disgusted by what he saw. He summed up his feelings when he said;

'It was the saddest chapter of my life to have found no gratitude for having risked our lives for the Fatherland daily under a thousand hazards. I am not ashamed to confess that I wept in those sad November days of 1918 when I had to give up my 'plane which had served me so loyally in many battles. With emptiness in my heart I took off my uniform and, on the verge of despair, faced an uncertain future.

Another component of *Jagdgruppe Nr 9* was *Jasta* 80b. Although the unit still had some Albatros fighters on strength as late as mid-August, OAW-built Fokkers eventually arrived, as shown here. This group of grim-faced pilots includes, from left to right, unknown, Ltn Kurt Seit, Oblt Gottlieb Rassberger, unknown and possibly Ltn Filbig. Seated on the wheel chock is Vzfw Otto Agne. Note the striped tailplane of the D VII at the extreme right of the photograph. According to Allied intelligence, the unit marking was in black and white
(A Imrie via HAC/UTD)

Bavarian *Jasta* 78 was based at Bühl, near Saarburg, in the Army Group 'A' sector, so it too was positioned to counter IAF raids. Although it produced no aces, the unit's pilots did claim several IAF bombers. At left is the CO, Oblt Reinhold Ritter von Benz, and at right Ltn d R Gerhard Ungewitter, who claimed a No 55 Sqn DH 9 on 13 August – the same day Benz was killed in D VII (OAW) 4461/18. The Fokker seen here may have been the machine of Vzfw Karl Kallmünzer, and it displays the unit colours of a blue fuselage with two white stripes ahead of the tail (the latter being out of view)

APPENDICES

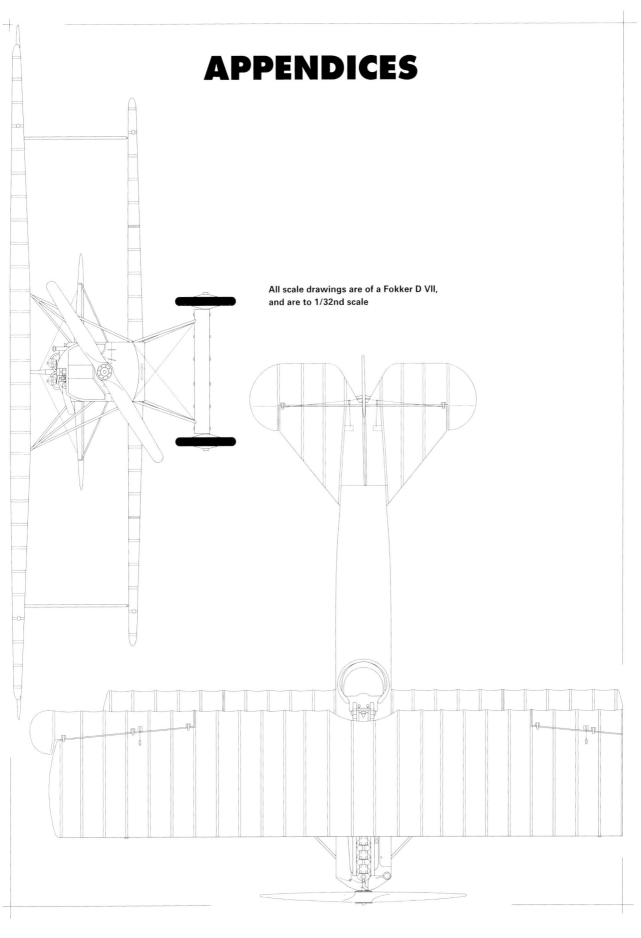

All scale drawings are of a Fokker D VII,
and are to 1/32nd scale

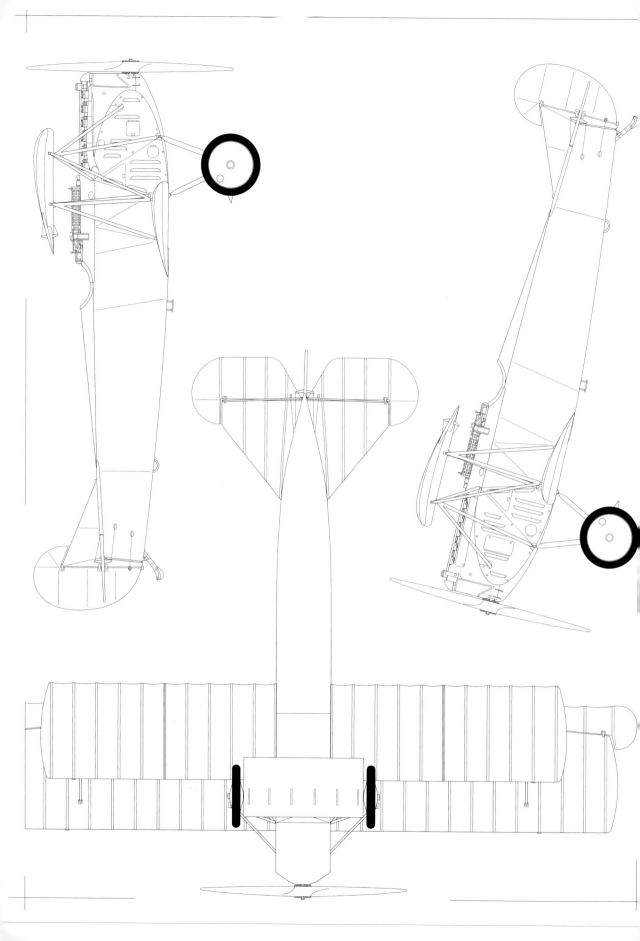

Artist Harry Dempsey has created the colour profiles for this volume, working closely with the authors to portray the aircraft as accurately as circumstances permit. Some of the illustrations are, admittedly, reconstructions based on limited evidence and are described as such, while the colours portrayed are often approximations at best. The pioneering work in this field carried out by Alex Imrie was of great value. The research of Dave Roberts, Ray Rimell, Manfred Thiemeyer, Dan-San Abbott, Volker Haeusler, JörnLeckschied and others was also beneficial.

1

Fokker D VII 365/18 of Ltn d R Josef Jacobs, *Jasta* 7, Ste Marguerite, July 1918

This is an early Fokker-built D VII (accepted on 18 May 1918) and powered by a Mercedes D IIIa engine. Its 'streaky' camouflaged fuselage has been painted over in *Jasta* 7's black colour. Jacobs flew 365/18 several times in June and presumably later. This illustration is based on an indistinct line-up photograph and Jacobs' own sketch of his Triplane insignia. The aircraft initially retained its printed fabric finish on the wings, but it was probably eventually painted all black, as were other Fokkers in this unit.

2

Fokker D VII (serial unknown) of Ltn d R 'Willi' Nebgen, *Jasta* 7, Ste Marguerite, July 1918

Nebgen was a *Jasta* 7 'near-ace' with four victories, and his fighter is an early Fokker-built machine painted entirely black on all surfaces except for the national and personal markings. His individual emblem is the green and white diagonal band on the aft fuselage. A largely illegible legend in white appears on the black portion of the fin (possibly *I R 133*).

3

Fokker D VII (Alb) of Ltn d R Carl Degelow, *Jasta* 40, Lomme, August 1918

In *Jasta* 40 the black fuselages were augmented by a white tail unit. Cabane and landing gear struts and wheel covers were also black. The wings of this Albatros-built D VII are covered in five-colour fabric, with blue rib tapes and a diagonal white stripe on the top wing to identify the *Staffelführer*. Crosses are of 4:5 proportions. The 'white stag' emblem displays golden yellow antlers and hooves.

4

Fokker D VII (Alb) of Ltn d R Willi Rosenstein, *Jasta* 40, Lomme, August 1918

This D VII is similar to Degelow's (No 3) except for the personal white heart insignia. Both machines have a tubular gunsight mounted in front of the cockpit. Rosenstein brought up the rear of the *Jasta* formation, and the top wing of his fighter displays a single chord-wise white stripe on centre-section, which no doubt acted as a formating mark.

5

Fokker D VII (Alb) of Vzfw Paul Groll, *Jasta* 40, Lomme, August 1918

Paul Groll was credited with four confirmed victories, scored in the summer and autumn of 1918 prior to his death on 7 October. This provisional depiction is based on the sketch of Groll's insignia, which appeared in Degelow's book as well as on customary *Staffel* marking practices. According to *Jasta* 40 member Adolf Auer, Groll's quartered emblem was red and white.

6

Fokker D VII (Alb) of Ltn d R Hermann Gilly, *Jasta* 40, Bisseghem, October 1918

At some stage in September or October 1918, the white tail marking of *Jasta* 40 was altered by the addition of narrow pinstripes. According to Auer, these stripes were dark blue. Gilly's D VII displays this version of the unit marking, together with his white swastika insignia.

7

Fokker D VII (Alb) of Ltn d R Ludwig Beckmann, *Jasta* 56, Rumbeke Ost, September 1918

Before Beckmann assumed command of the unit, the *Staffel* marking of *Jasta* 56 had comprised a blue-grey fuselage with a yellow nose and tail. Beckmann reportedly changed the yellow components to red. His own personal marking was originally a simple red band on the blue-grey fuselage, with the white 'snake-line' apparently being added later. The wings were covered in four-colour fabric.

8

Fokker D VII (serial unknown) of Ltn zur See Gotthard Sachsenberg, MFJ I, Jabbeke, October 1918

Sachsenberg flew this flamboyantly-decorated D VII both as leader of *MFJ* I and then as CO of the *Marine Jagdgeschwader*. The yellow and black markings are recorded in contemporary literature, and the single black stripe on each elevator is the *MFJ* I unit emblem. The upper wing seems to have been yellow on the uppersurface at least, while the remainder of the wings were covered in four-colour fabric. The black patches on the surface of the top wing are questionable. They were probably not intended as markings, as their location over the main and auxiliary spars indicates that they were part of some sort of crude fabric repair, with span-wise tapes applied across them to strengthen the fabric. This D VII apparently has a high-compression Mercedes D IIIaü engine, although the guns are mounted in the high position associated with the BMW installation.

9

Fokker D VII 5192/18(?) of Vzflgmstr Hans Goerth, MFJ III, Jabbeke, October 1918

This is a highly provisional illustration of the D VII in which Goerth claimed a victory on 1 October 1918, and is based on the description and sketch contained in his combat report. The report cites serial number 5192/18, which does not fit any known production list from any manufacturer. It is either mistaken or perhaps the number is derived from an unknown batch. The report describes the typical yellow nose and elevators, with the black heart on a white band as the pilot's personal markings. The wheel covers were probably yellow as well, and the three black stripes on the elevators reflect standard MFJ III identification as established by Gotthard Sachsenberg.

10
Fokker D VII (Alb) 838/18, Vzflgmstr Hans Goerth, MFJ III, Jabbeke, October 1918

Another speculative reconstruction, this scheme is also based on one of Goerth's combat reports. The document described the yellow elevators with three black stripes of MFJ III, along with the yellow nose and personal marking of a blue band edged in yellow.

11
Fokker D VII (OAW) 4499/18 of Vzflgmstr Franz Mayer, MFJ III, Jabbeke, September 1918

The combat report of Mayer's 5 September 1918 victory describes this machine as having a yellow cowling and elevators and a black and white striped fuselage. The three black stripes, which later characterised this unit, have probably been applied to the elevators, while the wings have been covered in four-colour fabric. Mayer scored at least two confirmed and one unconfirmed victories, but he is sometimes credited with four.

12
Fokker D VII 387/18 of Oblt Harald Auffarth, *Jasta* 29, Aertrycke, October 1918

Auffarth's combat report for 5 October 1918 mentions a yellow nose, green fuselage and his personal comet insignia. It also states that there were black and white markings on the underside of 387/18's fuselage, but the photograph does not provide details of these. The fighter's wings are covered in five-colour fabric and the aircraft has a Mercedes D IIIa 37254 engine.

13
Fokker D VII (Alb) 571/18 of Oblt Adolf Gutknecht, *Jasta* 43, Haubourdin, July 1918

The unit's marking consisted of white tails, with each aircraft showing an individual number on the fin. Befitting his status as CO, Gutknecht had '1' as his number, and the fighter's serial number was repeated in small characters beneath the tail as *Fok D VII Alb 571*. The fuselage displays personal black and white colours, and a white-bordered black stripe adorns the top wing. Cowling panels and wheel covers remain in factory finish green-grey, with four-colour fabric wings. Unusually, this Albatros-built D VII has OAW style lifting handles on the aft fuselage.

14
Fokker D VII (Alb) (serial unknown) of Ltn Josef Raesch, *Jasta* 43, Haubourdin, July 1918

This aircraft had been flown by *Jasta* 43's previous *Staffel* commander, Ltn Otto Creutzmann, prior to it being issued to Ltn Josef Raesch, and it still bears the former's personal emblem of a three-pronged *mistgabel* (manure fork) in recognition of his family's large livestock farm. Raesch, whose family were also farmers, decided to keep the insignia after inheriting the fighter. The colour of the nose is unrecorded – blue has been suggested, but red (or even black) is a

plausible choice. Considerable fabric repair is evident on the fuselage aft of the engine cowling. Four-colour fabric covers the wings and the number '2' appears on the white fin.

15
Fokker D VII 262/18 of Ltn Emil Thuy, *Jasta* 28, Ennemain, June 1918

An early Fokker-built machine, this D VII displays Thuy's personal white band on the streaky camouflaged fuselage. The crosses have been converted from a thicker format and a crudely patched installation for a flare pistol is visible beneath the cockpit. This D VII probably bears the unit marking of a yellow tailplane, with black stripes and five-colour fabric on the wings.

16
Fokker D VII (serial unknown) of Ltn Emil Thuy, *Jasta* 28, Mons-en-Chaussée, August 1918

This illustration is based on a photograph which apparently shows a later Fokker-built D VII flown by Thuy with a later-style national insignia and unusual rudder crosses. It displays the yellow and black *Jasta* tail markings and leader's streamers trailing from the interplane struts.

17
Fokker D VII (Alb) 6880/18 of Ltn Carl-August von Schönebeck, *Jasta* 33, Beuvry, October 1918

Von Schönebeck described the markings of his D VII for several historians – yellow nose unit marking with white numbers for individual identification (his was '7'). He also reportedly stated that his machine had a yellow tailplane as well. Four-colour fabric covers the airframe in this illustration.

18
Fokker D VII (OAW) 4025/18 of Ltn Paul Strähle, *Jasta* 57, Aniche, September 1918

Strähle's D VII is well-documented in both photographs and his own descriptions. The pale blue fuselage and tail represents the unit marking, with each pilot having his own nose colour. The red nose is matched by a red fuselage band to help identify the commander's machine, while the wings are covered in four-colour fabric.

19
Fokker D VII (serial unknown) of Ltn Hans von Boddien, *Jasta* 59, Emerchicourt-Nord, June 1918

This is a highly tentative identification, based on a very distant view of the machine in a line-up photograph in which it apparently displays a white nose and tail, with the pilot's personal 'B' emblem on a dark band with white outlines. The red colour depicted is based on an assumption. Von Boddien had previously served in *Jasta* 11.

20
Fokker D VII (OAW) 4598/18 of Ltn Josef Mai, *Jasta* 5, Villers-sur-Nicole, September 1918

Mai was flying this D VII in its famous 'dazzle' paint scheme when he scored his 26th and 27th victories. As usual, the wings remain in four-colour 'lozenge' fabric. There is a report that Könnecke flew this aircraft before Mai.

21

Fokker D VII (Alb) (serial unknown) of Ltn Georg Meyer,
Jasta **37, Neuville, October 1918**

Meyer's Fokker displays a personal insignia of a white fuselage sash with black borders, together with a black nose. The *Jasta* 37 marking of a diagonally zebra-striped tail is shown with a five-colour fabric finish.

22

Fokker D VII (Alb) (serial unknown) of Vzfw Oskar Hennrich, *Jasta* **46, Moislains, September 1918**

Staffel 46 commander Otto Creutzmann instituted the use of a black and white fuselage as unit marking. Hennrich's 'H' monogram is provisionally depicted as deep yellow, but it could also have been red or black. This machine has a BMW engine and a replacement lower wing from an OAW product. Four-colour fabric is used.

23

Fokker D VII (OAW) (serial unknown) of Oblt Hasso von Wedel, *Jasta* **24, Guise, October 1918**

This is another speculative illustration based on a partial photograph. Von Wedel used the *richtrad* from his family's coat-of-arms as an individual emblem, which was red on a white panel and is repeated here on top of the fuselage. This D VII may have also been powered by a BMW engine and had five-colour fabric.

24

Fokker D VII (OAW) 2052/18 of Ltn Karl Thom, *Jasta* **21, Boncourt, June 1918**

The *Jasta* 21 unit marking at this time was a wider version of the black and white vertical stripe which had been used since late 1916. Thom's personal marking, also seen on his Albatros fighters, was an angular black 'T' with a white outline. Fellow *Jasta* 21 ace Emil Thuy used a white arched 'T' to differentiate his Albatros machines. Thom's 'T' is repeated on both port and starboard upper wing surfaces, but without the white border. This marking may have also been applied in this form to the underside of the lower wing. The D VII's nose and tail are also painted black to act as personal identification.

25

Fokker D VII (Alb) (serial unknown) of Ltn Fritz Höhn, *Jasta* **21, Boncourt, August 1918**

'Balloon-buster' Höhn flew this highly-decorated Fokker which bore his 'H' on the fuselage sides and beneath the lower wings. The upper wing is provisionally depicted as decorated in the manner of Thom's machine. Many *Jasta* 21 D VIIs bore personal colours on nose and tail, in this case possibly black and white stripes.

26

Fokker D VII (OAW) (serial unknown) of Ltn Arnd Benzler, *Jasta* **60, Chémery, October 1918**

The Fokkers of *Jasta* 60 displayed unit décor of a black and white chequerboard on both surfaces of the tailplane. Benzler's mount is shown here personalised with a dark fuselage band (provisionally in red), edged in white. It has four-colour fabric and typical OAW-style camouflage on the engine cowling.

27

Fokker D VII (OAW) 4?98/18 of Ltn Karl Ritscherle, *Jasta* **60, Chémery, October 1918**

Ritscherle's D VII displays a black and white 'Mercedes Star' personal emblem on a white panel as well as the unit's chequerboard tail. Numerous colourful bullet hole patches are in evidence, along with crudely repaired fabric on the port fuselage side forward of the cockpit. The serial number is obscured but was probably either 4198 or 4498/18.

28

Fokker D VII (OAW) (serial unknown) of Ltn Walter Blume, *Jasta* **9, Sissone, September 1918**

Blume himself described how his aircraft featured a black fuselage, white nose and tail *Jasta* 9 unit markings and his personal 'B'. He also stated that the fighter's wings were white, which was an over-simplification. As depicted here, little more than half of the top upper wing surface back to a line stretching between the trailing edge of the cross insignia is white. A similar display may have been carried on the underside of the lower wing, which was covered in four-colour fabric.

29

Fokker D VII (OAW) (serial unknown) of Ltn Ulrich Könemann, *Jasta* **45, Arcy, July 1918**

This unit's *Staffel* markings seem to have consisted of a white tail section and dark-coloured nose, both with sharply diagonal demarcations. The cobalt blue nose colour shown here is entirely provisional. Könnemann's personal insignia is the black (possibly) and white fuselage band. This is an early-production OAW D VII in four-colour fabric, with 'hazy' purple and green camouflage patches on the cowling.

30

Fokker D VII (OAW) 2035/18 of Ltn Rudolf Windisch, *Jasta* **66, Monceau-le-Waast, May 1918**

Windisch was shot down while flying this new machine on 27 May 1918. The white stag insignia, like Degelow's, was based on the emblem of Dr Lahmann's Dresden Sanatorium at *Weisser Hirsch*. A combat report completed for the missing Windisch by Erich Sonneck describes the markings of 2035/18 as a 'white stag with a yellow coat of arms below'. No such yellow marking is visible in the photograph, so it is possible it appears on the fuselage underside. The aircraft is depicted in standard early D VII OAW finish of four-colour fabric.

31

Fokker D VII (Alb) (serial unknown) of Ltn Alfred Fleischer, *Jasta* **17, Vivaise, September 1918**

Jasta 17's unit marking in late 1918 was a white radiator shell and a black nose. This D VII displays personal markings in the form of stripes and a pennant on the five-colour fuselage, here conditionally depicted as yellow. A 'border' of the same colour is applied to the fuselage longeron positions, which may have extended onto the tailplane.

32

Fokker D VII (Alb) (serial unknown) of Ltn Günther Schuster, *Jasta* **17, Mars-sous-Bourcq, July 1918**

Schuster took command of *Jasta* 17 on 12 June 1918, and

downed a balloon on 15 July for his sixth, and final, victory. As commander, he flew this highly decorated D VII, which apparently had an all-black fuselage adorned with a white lightning bolt as a personal emblem. The tail may have been black as well, while five-colour fabric probably covered the wings.

33
Fokker D VII (serial unknown) of Vzfw Wilhelm Stör, Jasta 68, Preutin, September 1918

Jasta 68's unit badge was apparently the broad black and white bands applied to the aft fuselage of its D VIIs. Willy Stör – not to be confused with Heinrich Stör of Jasta 35b, as one of the authors previously did – displayed a white winged sword personal emblem. This Fokker-built machine has four-colour fabric and 'Fokker olive' cowling panels.

34
Fokker D VII (serial unknown) of Oblt Karl Menckhoff, Jasta 72, Bergnicourt, July 1918

No unit marking is known for this Staffel, but Menckhoff's machine is depicted here covered in four-colour fabric with his white 'M' on both the wing and fuselage. A D VII from the first Fokker production batch, this machine's wing and fuselage crosses show distinct evidence of conversion from an earlier style. It appears that the areas around those crosses was painted over in imitation of the lozenge fabric as part of the conversion process.

35
Fokker D VII 383/18 of Ltn Gustav Frädrich, Jasta 72, Bergnicourt, July 1918

Another early Fokker product, this aircraft seems to have been covered in five-colour fabric. As with Menckhoff's D VII, the metal cowls, axle wing and struts are in 'Fokker olive' finish and the crosses also display a similar conversion technique. This aircraft has a replacement OAW wheel cover on its starboard wheel, however. Frädrich's personal emblem was the black-bordered white band on the fuselage sides and top, as well as the upper wing.

36
Fokker D VII F 505/18 of Offz-Stv Wilhelm Hippert, Jasta 74, St Loup-en-Champagne, September 1918

This has to be one of World War 1's most flamboyantly-decorated fighters. Allied intelligence reported that Jasta 74's unit marking took the form of a blue nose for its D VIIs, making the chequered fuselage and tail an extreme example of personal decoration. Furthermore, the name Mimmi appears in ornate black and white characters on the four-colour top wing fabric.

37
Fokker D VII (Alb) (serial unknown) of Ltn Georg Weiner, Jasta 3, Mörchingen, September 1918

Although this D VII is thought to have been flown by Georg Weiner of Jasta 3, it is possible that he flew the fighter earlier while serving with Kest 3. His personal marking was the (possibly) black 'W' on a white panel with black borders. No unit markings are known, but the underside of the starboard lower wing has apparently been overpainted an unidentified colour. Four-colour fabric has been used to cover the machine.

38
Fokker D VII (Alb) (serial unknown) of Ltn August Raben, Jasta 18, Möntingen, October 1918

The four-victory commander of Staffel Raben flew a D VII marked in the now-famous unit colours. His is the only machine to bear a white raven on a vermilion red fuselage. The raven emblem has been applied with the same stencil as the usual black version, and it appears to be quite detailed. Uppersurfaces of both wings are red.

39
Fokker D VII (Alb) (serial unknown) of Offz-Stv Wilhelm Kühne, Jasta 18, Möntingen, August 1918

Kühne was photographed with this machine, and he presumably flew it occasionally. However, it seems he died in a different D VII, as this (or one like it) turned up at Saargemünd after the war. It displays typical red and white unit colours and a black (possibly) perforated 'sash' on the fuselage. The tailplane was a dark colour, being shown here as red.

40
Fokker D VII (OAW) (serial unknown) of Uffz Erich Mix, Jasta 54, Wallersberg, September 1918

As a Saxon unit, Jasta 54 displayed the state colours of green and white, applied in stripes to the tailplane. Mix's personal emblem comprised a skull and crossbones enclosed in what seems to be a 'U' on a possibly black band with white borders. This D VII has four-colour fabric and the usual OAW finish.

Bodenschatz, K, *Jagd in Flanderns Himmel.* Munich, 1935

Degelow, Carl, 'Reminiscences of *Jasta* 40' (translated by P Kilduff). *Cross & Cockade Journal,* Vol 12 No 3, 1971

Duiven, R, 'Das Königliche Preussische Jagdgeschwader II'. *Over the Front,* Vol 9 Nos 3, 4 and Vol 10 No 1, 1994-95

Franks, N, Bailey, F and Guest, R, *Above the Lines.* London, 1993

Franks, N, Bailey, F and Duiven, R, *The Jasta Pilots.* London, 1996

Grosz, P, *Windsock Datafile 9, Fokker D VII.* Berkhamsted, 1989

Hayzlett, Jan (translator), *Hunting with Richthofen* (translation of Bodenschatz, *Jagd in Flanderns Himmel*). London, 1996

Imrie, A, *Osprey Airwar 17 – German Fighter Units June 1917-1918.* London, 1978

Imrie, A, *Vintage Warbirds 16: German Army Air Aces of World War One.* Poole, 1987

Kilduff, P (ed), *Germany's Last Knight of the Air, The Memoirs of Major Carl Degelow.* London, 1979

Langsdorff, W (ed), *Flieger am Feind.* Gütersloh, circa 1935

Möller, Hanns, *Kampf und Sieg eines Jagdgeschwaders.* Berlin 1939

Neumann, G (ed), *In der Luft unbesiegt.* Munich, 1923

O'Connor, N, *Aviation Awards of Imperial Germany in World War I and the Men Who Earned Them,* Vols. 1 to VII. Princeton NJ and Atglen PA, 1988 to 2003

Puglisi, W (ed), 'Comments on German Staffels', *Cross & Cockade Journal,* Vol 3 No 3, 1962

Puglisi, W (ed), 'Portrait of a Pilot': Paul Strähle' – *Jasta* 57. *Cross & Cockade Journal,* Vol 12 No 3, 1971

Puglisi, W (ed), 'Raesch of *Jasta* 43'. *Cross & Cockade Journal* Vol 8 No 4,1967

Rimell, R (ed), *Fokker D VII Anthology Nos 1, 2 and 3.* Berkhamsted, 1997, 2000, 2002

Stark, R, *Die Jagdstaffel unsere Heimat.* Leipzig, 1932

Udet, E, *Mein Fliegerleben.* Berlin, 1935

Wenzl, R, *Richthofen-Flieger.* Freiburg, circa 1930

Zuerl, W, *Pour le Mérite-Flieger.* Munich, 1938

INDEX

References to illustrations are shown in **bold**. Plates are shown with page and caption locators in brackets.